'Careful biblical interpretation at its best: wisdom, insight, pathos,
challenge and encouragement – and all from one priceless book of
the Bible persuasively interpreted from beginning to end. Add to this
pearls of wisdom (dropped it seems, almost in passing) which helps us
to study the Bible better for ourselves, as well as insights which will
help us to live the Christian life more consistently – and here you have
a book of great value. *How God Treats His Friends* is a must-buy.'

Sinclair B Ferguson
Chancellor's Professor of Systematic Theology,
Reformed Theological Seminary, USA and
Preaching Associate, Trinity Church, Aberdeen, UK

'Bob's writing on Job is both theologically profound and insightfully
connected with Christian experience. In difficult personal
circumstances, I found his treatment of creatureliness and evil little
short of life-saving. You won't regret interacting with this book.'

Andy Gemmill
Director of the Pastors' Training Course,
Co-Director of the Cornhill Training Course, Cornhill Scotland

HOW GOD
TREATS
HIS FRIENDS

BOB FYALL

Foreword by Sinclair B Ferguson

Republished and reprinted by Tron Books, 2025
Copyright © 1995 by Bob Fyall
Cover artwork and design: Megan Hogarth

Previously published by:
Christian Focus Publishing Ltd

Geanies House, Fearn, Ross-shire

IV20 1TW, Scotland, Great Britain

First printing 1995

Paperback ISBN: 978-1-917493-08-6
ePub ISBN: 978-1-917493-08-6

Contents

Preface   7

Foreword to the 1995 Edition   11

Introduction   13

The Structure of the Book of Job   15

1. Is God the Author of Evil? || Job 1-2   17

2. Where Is God When It Hurts? || Job 3   31

3. When Counselling Does Not Help || Job 4-11   43

4. If It Is Not He, Then Who Is It? || Job 9   53

5. To Whom Can We Turn? || Job 19   63

6. Not Speaking What Is Right || Job 15-25   71

7. Where Can Wisdom Be Found? || Job 28   75

8. Trying to Tie Him Down || Job 32-37   85

9. The Grandeur of God || Job 38-39   93

10. The Enemy Unmasked || Job 40-41   103

11. The Vision Glorious || Job 42   115

12. Job Revisited   125

13. Preaching Job   135

Preface

I am delighted to introduce this new edition of *How God Treats His Friends* by my colleague and friend, Bob Fyall.

Bob's scholarly work on Job has been widely influential among biblical commentators, in particular for his treatment of the mysterious Behemoth and Leviathan figures, such that the writer of (in my view) the preeminent commentary of recent decades acknowledges that 'to Bob Fyall in particular my debt is considerable, both in exegesis and in illustrative material.'[1]

Bob's first love, however, is preaching. His greatest desire has always been to open the word of God for the people of God, and to teach and train others for that preeminent task in the church. Expanded from its original edition in 1995, this book shares the wonderfully pastoral nourishment of the message of Job in a lively, accessible format which is easily readable for any Christian as well as highly stimulating for any Bible teacher. Warm and insightful, erudite and encouraging – I know that all who read and ponder these pages will find much to enrich their own life and witness as they discover more of the wonderfully faithful way God treats his friends, as he leads them steadily to their ultimate blessing.

William J U Philip
Senior Minister, The Tron Church, Glasgow

---

1   Christopher Ash, *The Wisdom of the Cross* (Crossway, 2014), 441.

Foreword to the 1995 Edition

I have sometimes thought that it is one of the great 'treats' of life in the Christian church to have friends who combine special expertise in the study of the Old Testament with a commitment to share its riches. To read or listen to exposition which is sensitive to its literature, language, imagery and themes is a high privilege. It is to have the mind stretched to take in the sheer greatness of the covenant–making God, to have the will redirected to serve him, and, yes, to have the emotions cleansed. Those — like Bob Fyall — who are able to handle the Old Testament with such skill are among the treasures of the church.

Dr. Fyall is an Old Testament scholar who teaches at St. John's College, Durham and brings to his writing his considerable scholarly expertise. But more than that, in these pages he places his gifts at the disposal of non-experts like ourselves, and invites us to read through the book of Job with him, as friends. As we do so, we will soon feel that he is sitting beside us and — as a patient teacher — is pointing out many of the things he knows we need to learn, and asking us, 'Do you see this? And this? And this?' One indication of Bob Fyall's gifts is that when he points out things to you, they become hard to miss.

I think I can promise you that the experience of reading *How God Treats His Friends* will be very rewarding indeed. In his easy and pleasant style Dr. Fyall will show you wisdom, insight, pathos, challenge and encouragement — and all from one priceless book of the Bible.

The book of Job is a majestic piece of literature by any standard. But it is more; it is God's word, and with the help of these chapters you will at times be stunned by its power and find it speaking to you in a multitude of fresh ways.

How God Treats His Friends has many fine points. Perhaps the most important of them is that its interpretation of the book of Job is consistent and convincing. It would be wrong to steal a book's thunder, but perhaps it will whet your appetite to know that, unlike many commentaries and studies of Job, Dr. Fyall's exposition persuasively interprets it from beginning to end. Those who have read other works on Job may well find themselves saying as they come to the conclusion of this one, 'Now it is clear what the book of Job is about; it all makes sense; why didn't I see that before?'

A further strength should be mentioned. As someone whose interests lie in the world of the ancient Near East in which the Old Testament is set, Dr. Fyall is sensitive to the ideas, beliefs and concepts which were part of that paganly religious environment. He shows how the book of Job, like other biblical books, used the language and concepts of its day in the service of divine revelation. To some readers of the Old Testament this may be a new and strange concept to grasp. But in many ways it will underline the sheer power with which 'In the past God spoke to our forefathers' (Hebrews 1:1). The marvellous thing is that Bob Fyall deals with all this in a way that demonstrates how Scripture speaks to our own time and indeed to our own needs too.

These qualities alone would make *How God Treats His Friends* a must-buy. Careful biblical interpretation at its best is worth reading for its own sake. But add to this pearls of wisdom (dropped it seems, almost in passing) which helps us to study the Bible better for ourselves, as well as insights which will help us to live the Christian life more consistently - and here you have a book of great value.

'No-one who reads the book of Job can remain indifferent; it is an exhilarating if often bruising experience', writes Dr. Fyall. So prepare to be bruised and exhilarated as you turn these pages with your Bible beside you. As you read you will come to appreciate the book of Job in a new way; you will also want to read the Old Testament much more. And I suspect you will be on the look-out for another book from the same author. But until then, *How God Treats His Friends* will be worth re-reading!

Sinclair B Ferguson
Then of Westminster Theological Seminary, Philadelphia

Introduction

This is a second edition of a book first published by Christian Focus in 1995. It has gone out of print and I am very grateful for the invitation of Tron Books to have it reprinted. I have taken the opportunity to add two chapters: chapter 6 which is further comment on Job's Friends and chapter 13 which deals with preaching on Job. There are a few minor changes where I felt ideas could be expressed better and a small number of footnotes. Otherwise, the book is substantially the same as the earlier edition.

The earlier edition began life as a series of talks on Job given to Durham University Christian Union in January and February 1992. Much of the basic study for the book and the talks was done in preparation for my doctoral thesis on the imagery of Job for Edinburgh University which was submitted in 1991. A substantial revision of this thesis was published in 2002 by IVP as 'Now my eyes have seen you: Images of creation and evil in the book of Job' as part of their series New Studies in Biblical Theology. That book is a more technical work than the present volume and gives more detailed documentation for many of the ideas in *How God Treats His Friends*.

Over the years since this book was first published I have taught Job to students, first in St. John's College, Durham and then in Cornhill Scotland, Glasgow. I have appreciated many stimulating discussions and shared insights. Obviously I have changed my mind on this or that detail but remain convinced that careful interpretation of the imagery of the book culminating in a supernatural interpretation of Behemoth and Leviathan is the key to understanding Job. I trust this new edition will help people to appreciate the treasures of one of the most magnificent books in the Bible.

The first edition of this book was dedicated to my mother and to my father who had just died. Now that they are both with the Lord I acknowledge again those early days in a home where the Bible was loved and honoured. My chief debt is to Thelma, my wife of over forty years. She encouraged me as the early book was written and has made this edition possible by her love and support.

Bob Fyall
September 2025

The Structure of the Book of Job

The outline of the book is fairly straightforward and it is useful to have a good idea of the way the drama/debate develops.

1. Prose Prologue (Chapters 1-2)

First Test (Chapter 1) – Loss of family and possessions

Second Test (Chapter 2) – Loss of health and attack on sanity.

2. Poetic Dialogue (Chapters 3-41)

Introduction (Chapter 3) – soliloquy by Job on death and the loss of meaning.

First Speech Cycle (Chapters 4-14)

Eliphaz (Chapters 4-5) – Defence of traditional Wisdom teaching.
Job's First Reply (Chapters 6-7) – Both God and his friends have rejected him.
Bildad (Chapter 8) – God creates and governs justly.
Job's Second Reply (Chapters 9-10) – Legal disputation with God.
Zophar (Chapter 11) – God is unerringly just.
Job's Third Reply (Chapter 12-14) – Frailty and transience of humans and
                                       apparent arbitrariness of God.

Second Speech Cycle (Chapters 15-21)

Eliphaz (Chapter 15) – Questions Job's wisdom and innocence.
Job's Fourth Reply (Chapters 16-17) – Enmity and hostility of God.
Bildad (Chapter 18) – Fate of the wicked (i.e. Job)
Job's Fifth Reply (Chapter 19) – Plea to God to clear Job's name.
Zophar (Chapter 20) – Retribution comes to the wicked (i.e. Job)
Job's Sixth Reply (Chapter 21) – Fate does not always correspond to virtue.

Third Speech Cycle (Chapters 22-27)

> Eliphaz (Chapter 22) – God must be punishing Job for his sins.
> Job's Seventh Reply (Chapters 23-24) – Why does God allow injustice?
> Bildad (Chapter 25) – Sour tirade on God's power.
> Job's Eighth Reply (Chapters 26-27) – Mysteries of God's power and providence.

The Wisdom Poem (Chapter 28) – Interlude to evoke Wisdom.

Job's Apologia (Chapters 29-31) – Final statement of his integrity both personal and communal.

Elihu's Speech (Chapters 32-37) – Speculation on the place of suffering.

Yahweh's Speeches (Chapters 38-41)

> First Speech (Chapters 38-39) – Marvels of creation & providence.

> Second speech (Chapters 40-41) – Behemoth and Leviathan: images of evil.

3. Epilogue (Chapter 42)

Job restored and blessed (Chapter 42)

I

Is God the Author of Evil?

Job 1-2

Teresa of Avila[1] once went through a very long period of darkness and depression towards the end of which she had a vision of God. God said to her, 'This is how I always treat my friends.' "Then Lord", she replied, "it is not surprising that you have so few".

That grim jest is very much in the spirit of the book of Job and indeed much of the Old Testament. Over and over again we find a seemingly irreverent questioning of God and his purposes. The Psalms are full of expressions such as "How long, O LORD". The prophet Jeremiah contains some of the most bitter questioning of God in or out of the Bible. The most striking of these is Jeremiah 20:7: "LORD, you deceived me", where the word used for "deceived" is often translated as "seduced". This questioning of God is indeed characteristic of Jewish literature in general, surfacing, for example, in a lighter way in The Fiddler on the Roof: "Would it interrupt some vast eternal plan if I were a wealthy man?"

1 Teresa of Avila (1515-1582), a Spanish Carmelite nun, devoted to prayer and meditation.

But nowhere is this questioning more anguished or sustained than in the book of Job. The book is provocative and mind-bending. Many familiar certainties dissolve and, like a rider on a roller-coaster, the reader often wonders if the ground will ever be safely reached.

Job belongs to what is often called Wisdom Literature, along with Proverbs, Ecclesiastes and other parts of the Bible such as the Song of Songs and some of the Psalms (e.g. Psalm 1, 49, 73). The term 'Wisdom' is a wider concept in Biblical literature than the English word suggests. Thus in Exodus 31:3 Bezaleel, the maker of the Tent in the desert is called 'wise'; in Isaiah 40:20 and Jeremiah 10:9 craftsmen are so described and in Ezekiel 27:8-9 the term is applied to shipwrights. At the court of David it was used of political advisers such as Ahithopel and Hushai. The term thus has implications not only of intellectual understanding but of skill and grasping the right way to live. Wisdom is the art of living well in harmony with the principles on which God has made and runs the universe.

True wisdom belongs to God alone: "To God belong wisdom and power" (Job 12:13). That wisdom is at the heart of creation: "How many are your works, O LORD, in wisdom you made them all". (Psalm 104:24 NIV). It is the foundation of right living: "The fear of the LORD is the beginning of wisdom." (Proverbs 9:10). Yet the paradox of the book of Job is this: Job exemplifies wisdom, he has all the qualities the Bible commends and yet he is plunged into deep and black tragedy.

The structure of the book is that Job chapters 1 and 2 are an apparently simple story, a kind of traditional tale which is completed in Job 42:10-17. The bulk of the book is a magnificent poem running from Job 3:1-42:9. An outline of the book can be found on pages 15-16 and it would be helpful to refer to that from time to time.

The situation of Job creates the occasion for a debate — if debate is the right word — on the problems of evil and suffering. There is on one level a straightforward issue: is good rewarded and evil punished? But on a deeper level, the question is: can we trust, can we believe in, can we have confidence in the God who created the worlds? It is no accident that this question is explored in what is perhaps the greatest poetry in the Old Testament. Thus to respond to and appreciate the book, the reader must be sensitive to the imagery, the pictures and the whole dazzling cascade of ideas in what is arguably the Old Testament's greatest literary work.

To describe Job in this way is to draw attention to the fact that its profound message is embodied in equally great literature. The vivid and colourful imagery expresses the ideas in memorable ways. The sense of the vastness and mystery of the universe is not merely stated but visually captured in chapters such as Job 9, 26 and 38. Moreover the artistry is not simply eloquence, but extends to the finest details and the ideas are expressed with delicacy and verve. No-one who reads the book can remain indifferent; it is an exhilarating if often bruising experience.

Job chapters 1 and 2 raise, in an acute form, the question: is God the author of evil? When dreadful things happen; when cancer strikes the life of some young mother, who dies and leaves a husband and small children; when a tidal wave sweeps over and destroys an entire village; when war and violence tear apart communities; when appalling disasters come into our lives; is the blame to be laid for these on God's presumably broad shoulders? Is God the author of evil?

To explore this question from Job chapters 1 and 2 it is useful to examine the three main characters in the story: God, Job and Satan.

We shall look first at the individual who is the storm centre of these disasters; then at God himself who appears to be responsible for them; and finally at Satan who is the agent of Job's agonies.

Job

We begin then with Job himself. The author cleverly builds up a picture which makes him a human being rather than an Israelite. He lives in the land of Uz, possibly somewhere in the Arabian desert. The setting sounds patriarchal, but, unlike Abraham, Job is not given a family tree. The point of this is that Job is being presented as a representative of humanity as a whole, not specifically as an Israelite. Indeed it is characteristic of the Old Testament that many of the most important events of Israel's faith do not take place on Israelite soil. We may mention as examples the call of Moses, the giving of the Law and the stories of divine intervention in Ezekiel and Daniel. This underlines the fact that the message of the Old Testament is for the whole of humanity.

Now what kind of person is Job? It is significant that his character is mentioned before his wealth. He is "blameless" (Job 1:1), a word used of clean animals offered for sacrifice (e.g. Leviticus 1:3). He is also "upright" (Job 1:1), a word which suggests on the one hand that he is honest and open, and, on the other hand, a person who is generous and kind. He is "one who feared God", and this is the quality which Proverbs 1:7 describes as "the beginning of wisdom."

In other words, Job is presented as someone who exemplifies all the qualities of wisdom. He was also a widely known figure, mentioned in Ezekiel 14:14 and 20 along with Noah and Daniel. And he is held up for admiration in the Letter of James, "You have heard of the steadfastness of Job" (James 5:11). Now the point is not that he was sinless, not that he was perfect, but that he was genuinely good. Job is in no sense a hypocrite; his goodness is not superficial, he is genuinely good, genuinely caring, genuinely compassionate. Even Satan does not doubt that Job is good but he thinks that is only the case because of what he can get from God. In chapter 29 Job gives a fuller picture of his life before tragedy struck.

What we have in this story then is not suffering that comes as a result of wrongdoing or mistakes. If I crash my car into a brick wall at 100mph I will experience the consequences of my own stupidity if I am still alive to experience them. If we tell lies and cheat we will eventually be caught out, and so on. What we are dealing with here is a genuinely good person overwhelmed by a series of disasters for which he is in no way responsible.

This is emphasized by the fact that God calls Job "my servant" (Job 1:8). Now in the Old Testament the term 'my servant' is not simply used of pious individuals but rather of those who have a particularly close relationship with God. More especially it is used of Moses and the prophets and David. Then there is the powerful picture of the Servant in the later chapters of Isaiah. Thus what is happening to Job is a particularly devastating example of how God treats his friends.

The mystery is compounded by the fact that disaster strikes immediately after Job offers sacrifices and prayers for his family. Hard on the heels of his prayers, a series of hammer blows robs him of his family, his possessions, his health and almost his sanity. The way the story is told, the repeated "while he was yet speaking, there came another and said" (Job 1:16, 17, 18) speeds up the narrative and underlines the relentlessness of the catastrophes. These are heightened by the background of the peaceful scene of oxen ploughing and donkeys grazing. Suspense grows as we wait for Job's reaction. How is this man going to react to these awful events?

His first reaction comes in 1:21, "Naked I came from my mother's womb, and naked shall I return. The LORD gave and the LORD has taken away; blessed be the name of the LORD." Job, in the face of these disasters asserts that God is responsible for the whole of life.

His next reaction is, "Shall we receive good from God, and shall we not receive evil?" (Job 2:10). Now the word "receive" is not a particularly apt translation. What the Hebrew word suggests is 'shall we not actively cooperate with God in whatever he sends us?' Job is not saying we must grin and bear it. Rather he is saying that whatever happens we must continue to love God, trust him and keep on walking with him.

Thus the Job of chapters 1 and 2 is a person of enormous integrity, a person who is walking with God and fears him. In spite of this he is not only overwhelmed by a series of disasters, but experiences these immediately after praying that such things would not happen. Many have had an experience like that. They have prayed earnestly and with faith for something, believing God would grant it, and then found themselves face to face with the very situation against which they prayed and which they believed God would never allow to happen.

God

This brings us conveniently to our second point which is the part God plays in all this. Is God the author of evil? Now the Old Testament is not afraid in places to say just that. Amos 3:6 says, "Does disaster come to a city, unless the LORD has done it?" Even more striking is the stark statement of Isaiah 45:7 "I make well being and create calamity." But the big question is: does God create evil in the same direct way that he creates good? Does evil come from the hand of God in exactly the same way that good comes from the hand of God? Nor is this simply an Old Testament problem. John 1:3 reads, "All things were made through Him, and without him was not anything made that was made". That presumably includes the bad things as well as the good things.

What does the author of Job do in the face of this problem? What he does is to show that earthly events happen as a result of decisions made in heaven. This, however, does not imply a mechanical and deterministic universe. God is not like a machine operator who presses a series of switches and buttons which cause the machine to go in a totally predetermined manner. What the author presents is a far more dynamic picture, the picture of the heavenly court or council, the sons of God or angels who present themselves before God.

The idea of the heavenly court or council is a very common

one in the ancient world. Israel's Canaanite neighbours believed that the gods met in council on a mountain and the Greeks had a similar belief about Mount Olympus. Some Old Testament passages speak of a divine court.

Psalm 82 speaks of God standing in the council of the gods to give judgment. Another significant passage is 1 Kings 22:8ff. where Ahab, king of Israel and Jehoshaphat, king of Judah, ask the LORD for advice about whether to go and take the Syrian city of Ramoth Gilead. A prophet called Micaiah tells of a vision of the heavenly court, "I saw the LORD sitting on his throne, and all the host of heaven standing beside him on his right hand and on his left." In Isaiah 6 the prophet gives an account of his call, and in verse 8 of that chapter he hears the voice of the LORD speaking to his entourage, "Whom shall I send, and who will go for us?". The presence of the heavenly court is implied by the plural us and given tangible form by the presence of the seraphim. Thus there are the events on earth but these are orchestrated in heaven.

Now this helps to suggest at least the beginnings of a solution to the basic problem of the book of Job which, put succinctly is this: God is good, Job is innocent, and yet the calamities which come on Job come from the hand of God himself. The presence of the heavenly court establishes the uniqueness of God and his responsibility for what happens, for the other members of the court exist only in relation to him and derive their authority from him. Yet it also emphasizes the presence and activity of other powers in the universe. To put this another way: God is supreme, God is in control of what happens, but there are other powers in the universe which influence events.

This is a dramatic way of showing that God's creation, God's providence, is not mechanical, but involves a series of relationships and interaction between God and his creatures. This means that the answer to the question 'Is God the author of evil?' is not a simple 'yes' or 'no.' We shall continue to explore this basic question, not only in the rest of this chapter, but throughout the book.

That said, what are we to make of the fact that God actually incites Satan to move against Job? Satan comes into the heavenly court and God challenges him, "Have you considered my servant Job?" (Job 1:8). God throws down the gauntlet, as it were, and says, 'in all your comings and goings on the earth, have you seen such an outstanding example of faithfulness and integrity?'

It is necessary to nail Satan's accusation, "Does Job fear God for no reason?" (Job 1:9) because he is attacking not only Job's integrity but God's. This is seen when he goes on to say, "Have you not put a hedge around him and his house and all that he has on every side?" (Job 1:10). Is Job's faith simply a fair-weather one? Does he simply believe God when his family is flourishing, when his cupboard is full, when his flocks and herds are expanding and all is well. That, of course, is the big practical question which faces us so often. Is belief in God dependent on flourishing relationships, a good career, plenty of money and robust health.

Thus God in a very real sense is not just placing Job on the line but his own integrity as well. It is not enough to argue (as some have done) that since God knows what will happen, it is pointless to subject Job to these tests of faith. What Augustine pointed out long ago in relation to Abraham and Isaac is equally true of Job. Whatever God knew, Abraham certainly did not know that his faith was equal to the test. Likewise Job did not know, when these calamities struck him that he would emerge at the other end with his faith intact. Nor do the readers know this and hence the test is real. God is not going through a charade for his own amusement. Job's faith must be demonstrated not to be a fair-weather faith. It must be proved to Satan and indeed to the whole universe that Job does not simply fear God because God has blessed him.

Satan

We now look at the third main actor in the drama: Satan, or more accurately, since the Hebrew text has the definite article, "the Satan". The Satan is mentioned twice by that title elsewhere in the Old Testament. He occurs in 1 Chronicles 21 where he incites King David to number the people and thereby to place faith in armies and prestige rather than God. He is also mentioned in Zechariah 3 where he proceeds against Joshua the High Priest. The word, probably as a common noun meaning the 'accuser' also occurs in some of the Psalms. Here, however, in Job, the figure plays a more striking role.

Now this story is anything but naïve, and the more we read Job 1 and 2, the more subtleties and depths appear. God does indeed challenge Satan, that is true, but notice how quickly Satan replies. It is almost as if Satan had come to the heavenly court with the specific object of proceeding against Job.

Another detail worth noting is the deliberate word play on the phrases 'the hand of God' and 'the hand of Satan' (see Job 1:10-12; 2:5-6). Job is in God's hands and God allows him to be in

Satan's hands. In many ways this is the key to what is happening in the book. A large part of Job's agony is that he imagines God has turned hostile. Part of the problem of the book is that Job has this enemy in heaven who is trying to destroy him and very often Job confuses the enemy with God himself.

Now we can dodge the problem; we can say that while God gives permission he is not really responsible for what Satan does. The trouble is that in any society, in any kind of body or institution, the head of that enterprise must carry the can for the activities of subordinates who are permitted to behave in a particular way. The higher is ultimately responsible for the lower. In any case, God is far more in total control of the universe than any human can be of any earthly society.

What is happening in the book is a titanic struggle between the forces of good and evil, between God and Satan. Job has become the battle ground for that struggle, a struggle which is ultimately to find its climax in the Cross where another man does battle with this titanic enemy on our behalf. The Friends of Job fail to see this, they try to explain mechanically what is happening. Plainly, if we miss this supernatural dimension, this struggle between God and his enemy whose focus and battleground is Job himself, then we will miss what the book is really about.

Three observations are worth making. The first is that God is in control and Satan can operate only within the divine permission. Thus God says to Satan, "He is in your hand; only spare his life". We may compare this with Job 38:11 where he says to the sea, "Thus far shall you come, and no farther, and here shall your proud waves be stayed."

Now depending on our faith at any given moment, the fact that God is in control may cause us to thank him or to dread him. Probably all of us have had the kind of experience where the problem is not that we do not believe God is in control, but that we secretly do not trust God to work out a scenario which we will like. We do not doubt that God is in control, nor even that he has our best interests at heart. What we doubt is that he knows as well as us what our best interests are.

It is wonderful to feel that God is in control when things are going well, but when things go disastrously wrong, we sometimes feel as C. S. Lewis felt on the death of his wife that we are in the hands of a "cosmic sadist."[2] God seems hostile and the light has gone out of the sky. This is particularly the theme of Job 3 which we shall explore in the next chapter.

The second is that evil powers opposed to God are active in the universe. This is an area in which two extremes have to be avoided. The first extreme is obsession with spiritual evil and seeing the need for deliverance from situations which can be explained adequately by our own fallen nature. Not that the devil is not always ready to exploit our sin and weaknesses. The other extreme is to ridicule and reject any kind of demonic activity and attribute everything to natural temperament and circumstances.

In terms of Job the big question to ask is where does Satan go after chapter 2? Why does he not appear in the book again? My argument, to anticipate, is that he does appear in the book again; indeed he appears regularly in various guises, and that the tremendous picture of Leviathan in chapter 41 is in fact an

2   A Grief Observed, C. S. Lewis. p.26, Faber and Faber, 1961.

embodiment of the evil one himself, "the ancient prince of hell"[3] of whom Martin Luther speaks. Moreover, he so subtly imitates God that for most of the book Job imagines that the enemy who is attacking him is God himself. One of Satan's most dangerous devices is to speak with a voice that can be mistaken for God's own and act in a way that can be misunderstood as divine action.

The third observation is that all this is being experienced by a human being. The book is not merely someone speculating on the mysteries of existence and the problem of evil. This is a human being sitting on an ash heap in harsh and bitter agony and loneliness. The book of Job is an enormously practical book. It is a facing up to the existence of dark, sinister cosmic forces which are opposed to God and his gospel. To understand it, more than theology is needed, though we do need that; more than clear thinking is needed, although that is necessary as well. But above all faith, courage, and open and teachable spirits are needed as we explore this great book together.

3   In his hymn, "Eine feste burg."

2

Where Is God When It Hurts?

Job 3

With Job 3 we are plunged into an altogether more sinister world where dark cosmic crosscurrents are flowing. This introduces us to a reality which we will need to grapple with and of whose power we need to be aware. This is more necessary because there is a kind of Christianity which advocates that our lives should always be filled with laughter and happiness, and our worship always filled with praise and light-heartedness; the kind of Christianity that would have had Jesus singing a chorus at the grave of Lazarus. Not that joy, exuberance and happiness are wrong; far from it, they are a necessary part of our living and worship.

Nevertheless, these do not make up the whole of life and especially they do not address the question raised starkly by Job 3, 'where is God when it hurts?' There are times when it does hurt and hurt badly. If you are suffering from depression or the effect of some disaster, if you feel that God has abandoned you, what are you to do when confronted with this kind of hyped-up, triumphalist Christianity?

In this bleak and powerful poem Job eventually breaks the seven-day silence and expresses his feelings and agony in a tremendous soliloquy. The dialogue proper has not yet begun. Job has not yet begun to engage with his Friends and they have not yet begun to reply.

There are two initial comments to be made. The first is this: the experience of depression and suffering does not mean that God is angry with us. The Bible, the New Testament as well as the Old Testament, shows that those who walk most closely with God are often those who go through the deepest and darkest circumstances. The book of Jeremiah, for example has a passage almost identical to part of this chapter, where the prophet, like Job, also curses the day of his birth (Jeremiah 20:14-18). Many of the Psalms are called 'Lament Psalms,' the bleakest of these is Psalm 88 which not only begins but ends in darkness. Remember that these psalms were part of the worship of the Temple and an important element of Israel's faith. In 2 Corinthians Paul reveals much of the agonies he suffered and in particular his persistent 'thorn in the flesh' (2 Corinthians 12:7) which he had begged the Lord to take away. The supreme example, however, is our Lord in the Garden of Gethsemane when "he began to be greatly distressed and troubled" (Mark 14:33) and on the Cross where he cried "My God, my God, why have you forsaken me?"

This theme is also to be found throughout Christian literature, as witness the following two examples. In The Dark Night of the Soul, a book about the life of prayer, St. John of the

Cross[1] expresses it vividly:

> *"God sometimes attacks the soul in order to renew it and thus*
> *to make it God-like, and stripping it of the habitual affections*
> *and attachments of the old personality to which it is very*
> *closely united, destroys and consumes the spiritual substance,*
> *and absorbs it in deep and profound darkness."*

A similar emphasis occurs in many of the poems of Gerard Manley Hopkins,

> *"O the mind, the mind has mountains,*
> *cliffs that fall, frightful, sheer,*
> *No man fathomed.*
> *Hold them cheap, may they who ne'er hung there."[2]*

The sentence, 'Hold them cheap may they who ne'er hung there' is most important. The Friends, as we shall see, have 'ne'er hung' where Job is hanging and thus are incapable of empathising with him.

The reference to Hopkins leads to the second comment on Job 3 which is that it is a poem, indeed it is the beginning of the long poetic section of the book which now rolls its majestic way to Job 42:6. This means we must respond to it as a poem. It is not enough to take a concordance and look up every reference to darkness and clouds, still less to take a book on meteorology, read the sections on clouds and imagine we have understood this chapter. It must be received as a great poem. Poetry is not a flowery way of saying something which can be

1   St John of the Cross was a Spanish monk (1542-1591); the book was written in 1578 or 1579.
2   Gerard Manley Hopkins (1844-1889) was an English poet who went through many times of depression which he explored in a group of five poems called the Dark or Terrible Sonnets.

said just as effectively in prose. Poetry is a way of expressing the most intense and powerful emotions in the most intense and compelling way. Thus the distress of Job, and indeed of all who suffer, in this poem of immense and compelling power.

In our analysis of this chapter, I want to ask three questions. First, what is the nature of Job's distress, what is actually happening to him? Second, what are the reasons for the experience expressed in the poem? Third, is there a cure for his distress? A cure, that is, suggested by the chapter itself, rather than jumping to the end of the book.

What Is the Nature of Job's Distress?

The answer is not a straightforward one because many things are happening to him. The first is that his mind and emotions are filled by the thought of death. Indeed the theme of death is arguably the dominant one in the book, mentioned as it is in every one of the 42 chapters. Nor is this simply the death of individuals, because although Job has lost his family he does not mention them in this chapter. Rather death is seen as a dark power shadowing the whole of existence. The universe appears to be dominated not by God but by death, which stands as the ultimate question mark over against the goodness of God. The problem is a universal one.

These feelings of Job are expressed in powerful and colourful images. First of all Job thinks of death as a kind of womb to which he wishes to return. This image has already occurred in chapter 1 verse 21, "Naked I came from my mother's womb, and naked shall I return." The womb and death are the two terminal points and between these are a few years of misery.

Then Job thinks of what might be called the 'geography' of the underworld and his mind is filled with Sheol. the Hebrew name for the world beyond the grave. It is unfortunate that many English translations do not use this word but translate it simply as 'grave' or 'death.' Sheol was thought of as a dim, insubstantial, shadowy place where all activity and all the relationships that mark the world as we know it ceased.

Job also thinks of death as a place of blackness and shadow, "Let gloom and deep darkness claim it" (Job 3:5). The term 'deep darkness' is sometimes translated as 'shadow of death' and is best known from Psalm 23:4 where the psalmist speaks of walking through 'the valley of the shadow of death.' Above all, Job thinks of death as a hostile presence, an evil spirit dominating his horizon.

But not only are Job's horizon, personality and emotions dominated by death, he is also suffering from what we might call a kind of nihilism; his whole familiar world has simply dissolved around him. There is no longer any meaning and purpose, as the book of Ecclesiastes asserts, everything is vanity, futility, emptiness. The very basis of existence is questioned by Job — what is the point of it all?

Few of us have not been faced with that question. What is the point of going on? Sometimes this is expressed in more colloquial ways: it will all be the same in a hundred years time! We often speak and think what Job, in a much profounder and more poetic way is expressing in this chapter.

And indeed Job goes further, he wants the whole of creation to be dissolved, the cosmos to dissolve into chaos, the tape to be wound back. If verses 3-10 are read carefully and compared with

Genesis 1, Job is wishing that ancient chaos would return and that it would swallow up the ordered cosmos. At the beginning God had said "Let there be light," Job says "May gloom and deep darkness claim it." Genesis 1 is full of vibrant life: the life of animals, birds, fish and, of course, the life of humanity itself. Job 3 is full of death. And instead of the Sabbath rest of God satisfied with his work, there is the false rest of Sheol, the dead peace of the graveyard.

Now because of this sense of nihilism, because of the domination of his thoughts by death, Job has totally lost his zest for living. Job is not going through a bad patch, something far more profound is happening to him. Anyone who feels like this knows that being told to get a grip of oneself is simply adding a further cruel pressure. To speak like this is like telling someone with a broken leg to get up and run around. The one thing a person in Job's situation cannot do is get a grip on himself.

This is strikingly illustrated by verses 21-22 where Job expresses his passionate desire to break into Sheol the way a grave robber breaks into a tomb. We know from ancient Egypt and elsewhere that there was a profitable trade in grave robbing because of the possessions buried with the dead, but nowhere else does anyone wish to break into Sheol itself. A further illustration of this mood comes from the poetry of the First World War in the poem Futility by Wilfred Owen. In that poem, a young soldier's body lies on the ground in the early Spring sunshine, and the poet muses about his early days when the sun wakened him every morning, even in France, and he ends the poem,

> "O what made fatuous sunbeams toil,
> To break earth's sleep at all?"

Why did the sun bother setting the whole panorama of life into motion? Thus the nature of Job's distress is that he is dominated by death and nihilism and his zest for living has totally gone.

What Are the Reasons for These Feelings of Despair?

Why has Job apparently lost the robust faith of 1:21, "The LORD gave, and the LORD has taken away; blessed be the name of the LORD," and the equally robust 2:10, "Shall we receive good from God, and shall we not receive evil." Why has he now plunged into the depths of nihilistic despair?

The first reason is this: the utter silence of his Friends. The last verses of chapter 2, which will be examined later, speak of Job's three Friends, Eliphaz, Bildad and Zophar. They come to see him, but very far from comforting him, they treat him as if he were a dead person already. They carry out the rituals of tearing clothes and sprinkling dust which are normally associated with death. They sit and mourn for seven days, and from other parts of the Old Testament we know that this was the common period of ritual mourning. Joseph mourned for his father Jacob for seven days (Genesis 50:10); the people of Jabesh Gilead mourned for King Saul, their former saviour, for seven days (1 Samuel 31:13).

Can you imagine the effect of this on Job? Already crushed and broken, now his Friends treat him as if he were already dead, a person without hope and without a future. Now there is a time for silent sympathy. Sometimes when peoples' hearts are broken, the best thing to do is simply to sit and hold their hands. But there is also a silent bankruptcy when the silence does not arise from empathy but from having nothing helpful to say.

This, I suggest, is what is happening here: the Friends do nothing, they do not communicate. And this is why the opening words of chapter 3 are so important, "After this, Job opened his mouth." This is not simply saying that Job is speaking; it means rather that he was about to say something of significance. The Jerusalem Bible captures the idea effectively by paraphrasing the expression, "Eventually it was Job who broke the silence".

There is, however, a second element, at a deeper level than the silence of the Friends, namely, the activity of Satan himself. We have noticed that some commentators argue that Satan's activity ceases at the end of chapter 2 and that he simply disappears, his task done and he does not feature again. The argument of this book, which will be developed in later chapters, is that Satan does not disappear but rather changes guise. Here, in chapter 3, he is already at work filling Job's mind with images of darkness and chaos. We have here the first mention of Leviathan (Job 3:8), the sea monster and symbol of darkness and evil.

The atmosphere here is rather like that of Shakespeare's Macbeth where the witches fill the mind and dreams of Macbeth with images of blood, death and destruction. Similarly in chapter 7 and elsewhere Job talks about being tormented by dreams and visions. Now what is this all about? One of the ways the Old Testament, in poetic passages, speaks of creation, is in terms of a battle with the powers of chaos. This theme will be developed in later chapters but a brief comment is necessary here.

Israel's neighbours in the ancient world had many myths about a god of order and cosmos destroying a god of chaos and destruction. This was usually related to the creation of the world and associated with the raging waters. In Babylonian mythology Marduk destroyed Tiamat the evil power. Israel's nearest neighbours, the Canaanites, told their sagas of Baal, the champion of the gods, fighting the sea god Yam and the monster Lotan, the Canaanite equivalent of Leviathan. This is not to suggest that the Old Testament revelation is on the same level as the ancient myths, rather that ideas and stories familiar to the people of the time were being used to embody truths; similarly Paul quotes Greek poets to the philosophers in Athens (Acts 17:28).

And there are many places in the Old Testament where God's creation of the world is linked with the smiting of hostile powers. One of the most striking of these is Psalm 74:12ff. In these verses the ordered creation and the rhythm of the seasons is paralleled by "You crushed the heads of Leviathan".

This dimension of supernatural evil must be taken seriously. Job is here experiencing what Paul speaks of in Ephesians 6:12, "For we do not wrestle against flesh and blood, but against the rulers, against the authorities, against the cosmic powers over this present darkness, against the spiritual forces of evil in the heavenly places." The Satan of chapters 1-2 has unleashed spiritual forces against Job whose whole personality has become a battleground.

But there is a third reason, deeper still, why Job is suffering this distress: it is the sickening feeling that God has turned against him. Verse 20 in most of the versions and translations read, "Why is light given to him who is in misery?" This obscures the fact that the Hebrew text says "Why does he (i.e. God) give light?" Job is placing the blame fairly and squarely on God.

Then again in verse 23, "God has hedged in." God's presence

is no longer seen as protection but as claustrophobia. Job has lost confidence in God's good purposes for him. This is also a real problem for Christians, particularly for those who have been on the journey for some time. Often when people become Christians their lives are filled with peace and joy and God seems very close. But then sometimes he appears to withdraw, and not just withdraw but actually turn against us, and that is one of the hardest and most poignant experiences we can ever have. C. S. Lewis powerfully expresses this feeling:

> "Meanwhile, where is God? This is one of the most disquieting symptoms. When you are happy, so happy that you have no sense of needing him, so happy that you are tempted to feel his claims on you are an interruption, if then you remember yourself and turn to him with gratitude and praise, you will be welcomed by him with open arms. But go to him when need is desperate, when all other help is vain, and what do you find? A door slammed in your face, and the sound of bolting and double-bolting on the inside. After that silence, you may as well turn away. The longer you wait, the more emphatic the silence becomes. There are no lights in the windows; it might be an empty house. Was there ever anyone in it?"[3]

Much of what Job says in the rest of the book is related to this agony, this feeling that God has turned against him.

---

3   A Grief Observed, p.7.

Is There a Cure for Job's Distress?

If what has already been said about chapter 3 was all there was to say it could justifiably be accused of filling us with bleakness and despair, or at least reminding us of the bleakness and despair we would prefer to forget. What do we have to place against this? We must avoid the temptation to jump to the end of the book, our concern here is to see if there are any gleams of light in the chapter itself. I think two things can be said at this stage.

The first thing is in verse 20, God gives light. Now, as we have seen, the fact that God gives light causes Job enormous distress at this stage. But this is also to be Job's healing, because what has changed between chapters 2 and 3 is not the fact that God gives light but the way Job feels about that fact. Job's feelings about God have changed, but the reality of who God is has not changed. Nor has it changed when we ourselves run up against these dreary black times when God appears to have abandoned us, when the powers of darkness are having a field day and when our friends seem at best indifferent and at worst hostile. Then we have to cling to the great unshakeable certainties that God loves, that Christ died, that Christ is risen, that Christ will come again. It is these truths, not our changing feelings about them which are our security.

The second ray of light is Job's utter honesty. This is important in two respects. First of all it is important in relation to his thinking and feeling about death. We would do well to remember this too: that we are mortal and that the final truth about our lives and God's purposes can never be realised fully in this world. The final word on an individual can never be the one that is spoken during one's earthly life.

A missionary returning from long years of hard work in central Africa many years ago in the days of President Roosevelt, happened to travel across the Atlantic on the same ship as the President. Naturally enough when the ship landed there was great excitement and an enormous welcoming party for the President. By contrast there was no-one at all to welcome the missionary and his wife. That night in a very modest guest house they would not have been human if they had not felt neglected and upset, so as they prayed they said to God, "Lord surely there might at least have been someone to welcome us when we arrived home". And the Lord replied, 'But you're not home yet'. The final welcome and answer is in the world to come.

The second feature of Job's honesty is that it allows God to be honest with him. Not that God is ever dishonest with us, but sometimes we set up all kinds of evasions and subterfuges as we try to avoid the truth and thus avoid him. Job, in contrast to his Friends, realises the supernatural depths of the problem, and thus God is able to begin the painful process of healing. We need to wrestle with these problems as well and explore the depths with Job. And as we explore these depths, if we have the honesty and courage, it will be the doorway for us to meet God in a deeper and fuller way as well.

3

When Counselling Does Not Help

Job 4-11

In one of the '*Peanuts*' cartoons, Lucy says to Charlie Brown, "There is one thing you are going to have to learn: you reap what you sow, you get out of life what you put into it, no more and no less." Now Snoopy the dog who is in the corner of the cartoon doesn't like this much and he mutters, "I'd kind of like to see a little margin for error." Job's Friends admit of no margin for error, nor will they allow any deviation from what they see to be the norm.

Having examined the catastrophes which befell Job in the first two chapters, and seen his numbed depression in chapter 3 we realise that if anyone ever needed counselling and support, Job was that man. This is what his Friends come to do and yet they merely increase his depression. It is not that counselling itself is invalid, but their kind of counselling makes Job's situation far worse.

In this chapter we will look at their personalities in general and what they say in the early speeches. In chapter 6 we shall examine their later comments.

They are like a group of church leaders to whom Oliver Cromwell, having found them to be immovably stubborn, exclaimed in exasperation, "I beseech you in the mercies of Christ, think it possible you may be mistaken." Job's Friends never consider that they might be mistaken — it never crosses their minds that they might be wrong.

The Friends appear to stand comfortably within the mainstream Wisdom tradition with its view that the life of the righteous leads to prosperity and happiness. They fail to realise what the Wisdom literature actually teaches, namely that when the book is written, when the final dot is placed on the page, that the life of the just has led to the perfect day. It does not say anywhere in the Wisdom books that there will be no disasters and tragedies en route.

In Psalm 1, for example, which is a concise summary of what Wisdom is about, the life of the just is compared to a fruit-bearing tree planted by a river. There is no suggestion that there will not be storms or that the tree will not be attacked by worms; it is simply said that the tree will produce fruit. What the book of Job does is to fill in the picture, to explore the implications of the attacks made on the life of the just.

The three Friends are not sharply differentiated and there is a certain artificiality in trying to write character studies of them. Nonetheless they do have certain features which give them a measure of individuality.

Eliphaz is essentially a philosopher. His characteristic phrases are, "we have examined" and "I have observed". He is the kind of person we have all met; the kind of person who knows it all. Whatever you do, whatever you have seen, wherever you have been, he has done it or seen it or been there before you, and if he hasn't it's because it is not worth doing or seeing or visiting.

Bildad is a traditionalist, "For inquire, please, of former ages, and consider what the fathers have searched out" (Job 8:8). Tradition is, of course, important; we neglect what has been said and done in the past at our peril. The trouble with Bildad is that he locates all wisdom and insight in the past and ignores what God is doing now. He also shows vindictiveness, describing Job's words as "a great wind" (Job 8:1).

Zophar is a dogmatist and theorist. Even when he speaks of "the deep things of God" (Job 11:7) he is criticizing Job's lack of knowledge not his own. Thus he assumes that he does not need to listen to Job but simply belabour him with increasingly bitter denunciation.

What we are to consider is why the Friends fail as counsellors. This is helping us to explore the positive ways in which help can be given. In particular there are four ways in which the Friends fail to counsel adequately and which point beyond themselves to genuine spiritual counselling.

The first thing about the Friends is that *they have a simplistic and mechanical view of God.* They take ideas about God, about creation, about the world which are not wrong in themselves but they apply these in a rigid and insensitive way. For the situation of Job, as for every other, they have a ready made answer. Eliphaz, for example, says, "You shall come to your grave in ripe old age, like a sheaf gathered up in its season" (Job 5:26).

This is, of course, what happens at the end of the book. But this does not mean that we can simply jump to the happy ending, scurrying from chapter 2 to chapter 42 as if nothing had happened in between. Both Bildad and Zophar argue that since the kind of disasters in chapter 1 do not happen to good people, then Job cannot be good. He must be a secret sinner. Now there are two particular ways in which the Friends have a simplistic and mechanical idea of God.

First of all they have no place in their thinking for a developing relationship with God. This is in effect another way of saying that there is no place for a relationship at all, because you cannot have a relationship that does not develop. The Friends appear to speak all the commonplaces of orthodox theology while Job often speaks apparently blasphemous words. Yet God says to the Friends, "You have not spoken of me what is right, as my servant Job has" (Job 42:7) — God says exactly the opposite of what we might expect. Yet Job refuses to let go of Yahweh. Like Jacob in Genesis 32 he wrestles with God and refuses to let go until he has received a blessing.

The basic problem in our minds, faced with language of raw hurt and anger is that we think that God is not big enough to handle this kind of thing. We think that God is so delicate, so naïve and unsophisticated that he cannot handle this kind of anguish. We also naively think that if we only *feel* that way and do not express it in words, God will not know how we are feeling.

Now, of course, once we put this in words, we realise that it is nonsense. Yet there persists in us the feeling that God has to be cocooned and cottonwooled. In fact we treat God as if he were like some fragile maiden aunt who would collapse if we talked of something outside her limited experience. This comes out in different ways in our hymnbooks of all traditions and styles. We major on praise and joy which is right and good in itself. But how many lament psalms, for example, do we sing?

Thus the Friends do not realise that it is possible to have a developing, at times even an angry relationship with God. But this is true in human relationships. If a relationship goes sour, the way to put it right is not to pretend that nothing has gone wrong. It is usually by hot and angry words that the quarrels of lovers are settled. Pretending that everything is all right simply creates a tense, unreal situation which results in a worse break-up of the relationship.

The other way in which they have a mechanical and simplistic idea of God is that they have no realization of the dark mystery at the heart of creation itself. Eliphaz urges Job to put his case before God (Job 5:8), but Job's basic problem is that he is not certain that God will listen to him. This is well illustrated in 7:17 where Job says, "What is man, that you make so much of him, and that you set your heart on him?" This is a devastating parody of Psalm 8 where God's care of humanity is seen as a reassuring and strengthening fact. Job does not want care and attention, he wants to be left alone. Thus the Friends because of their simplistic and mechanical view of God's providence, do not realise that it is in fact Job's relationship with God which is plunging him into depths of agony and despair.

The second main reason why they fail to be good counsellors is that, like many since, *they imagine they can put God's case better than God.* They appoint themselves as his spokesmen almost as if they don't trust him to make his own case. Much of what they say, taken in isolation, is good and some of it is echoed by God in chapters 38ff, but they are blind to the mystery of God's creation. They do speak of creation and of how important it is to be humble before God, none of which Job disputes, but they miss the point.

Eliphaz in 5:9 says that God "does great things and unsearchable, marvellous things without number". Job does not doubt that; it is the good intentions of God that he doubts. The idea that God is all-powerful fills him with dread, because in his state of mind he fears this will almost certainly mean further misfortune.

Too often, people facing bitter agony and crushing sorrow have simply been beaten into subjection by those who come and tell them rather smugly that 'all things work for good to those who love God' (Romans 8:28). What is forgotten is that for Paul this hard-won confidence comes at the end of his exposition of the glories of the gospel. This is not said to someone who is in agony and trying to hold on to some rags and tatters of their faith; this is said by someone who is himself grappling with the mystery and darkness of creation.

Not only are the Friends impervious to the majesty of God's creation, they are also blind to God's grace. Essentially they hold the view that righteousness leads to prosperity. Today the baneful influence of prosperity theology has deeply infiltrated the church. To put it simply, this kind of theology maintains that if you trust God you will be wealthy, have a good job, a fine house and a large car, you will marry the right person, your children will be wonderful and your material prosperity will prove to the world that God is pleased with you. In other words God is a bargainer who treats people on a market basis. Grace goes out of the window and a market economy takes over where the rich, powerful and successful become the children of the kingdom and the downcast and the oppressed are excluded. Essentially what the Friends are saying to Job is that if he had been genuinely godly his prosperity would have remained.

This imagining that we can make God's case better than God is, of course, the oldest sin in the book. In Genesis 3 that is exactly what Eve did in the Garden of Eden when the serpent tempted her. Eve said that they were allowed neither to eat or touch the tree. In fact God had said nothing whatever about touching the tree. Eve was making God appear to be strict and tyrannical in order to disobey him. She made "his love too narrow by false limits of our own."[1] God is misrepresented as someone who bargains rather than one who is full of grace.

The third reason the Friends fail as counsellors is that *they do not listen*. The impression given by reading the speeches in the book of Job is that they all come along with prepared speeches which they are going to deliver whatever happens. All with experience of academic or church meetings know how common this is! This is illustrated by the fact that the debate appears to grind to a halt after chapter 25. Zophar does not speak at all; Bildad is uncharacteristically brief, and Eliphaz has fallen silent at the end of chapter 22. Some commentators argue that we have here a dislocation of the speech cycle and try to rearrange the text among the speakers. I will comment further on this in the discussion of chapter 28, but at the moment it is enough to say that the debate grinds to a halt because they have nothing else to say.

First of all they do not listen to God. They imagine that they have within themselves all the resources that are required and thus need no new relationship with God. An apparent exception is Eliphaz' dream (Job 4:12-17) where he speaks of a spirit who spoke to him "Amid thoughts from visions of the night, when deep sleep falls on men" (Job 4:13). This has often been taken as

---

1   From the hymn, 'There's a wideness in God's mercy' by F. W. Faber.

a description of inspiration, but a number of hints suggest that it may in fact have been a brilliant deception by the Evil One. In description of prophetic calls (e.g. Isaiah 6 and Revelation 1) there is indeed fear and trembling but there is also reassurance and blessing. Moreover, the message, "Can mortal man be in the right before God? Can a man be pure before his Maker?" (Job 4:17), because it is unexceptional, scarcely needs revelation from a spirit. There is no hope, no way forward, simply judgment and condemnation.

And that failure is highlighted in another basic failure in counselling. One of the most important lessons to learn in trying to help someone in distress is to take their problem with the utmost seriousness. We may privately believe that their perception is wrong, and we may be right, but in order to help we have to begin with people where they are. The Friends come to Job with their minds made up and thus they are no help to him. Eliphaz rejects anything that does not fit in with his preconceived ideas. Bildad rejects anything that has not been said in the past. Zophar is so fixed in his dogmatism that he has no room for new insights.

But not only do they fail to listen to God, they do not listen to Job in his agony. This becomes increasingly so as the debate continues. However, it is present from the beginning; Bildad describes Job's words as "a great wind" (Job 8:1); Zophar condemns Job's words as "babble" (Job 11:3).

We ourselves often fail to listen to the message of suffering. We judge books by whether they make us feel good, we judge worship by whether it makes us happy and we judge people by whether we find them fun and so on. Now that is not to say that it is wrong to read books which make us feel good, nor bad to have worship which is happy, nor enjoy the company of amusing people.

What is true is that if all our attention is devoted to these areas we will be like the Friends of Job and miss deeper dimensions about God, about suffering and about death. We must listen to God's voice when he speaks through suffering, "God's megaphone" as C. S. Lewis called it. So often, in the normal business of our lives, the voice of God is faint just as tuning into a particular channel and we hear faintly and far away the music from another channel. Sometimes that music can become very loud, and sometimes on a personal, community, national or global level, God's megaphone can no longer be ignored and we must listen to what he is saying.

And that brings us to the fourth reason why Job's Friends fail as counsellors; they fail because they do not discern that supernatural forces are at work. That is not to say that all suffering and agony comes from the devil, but we must be open to that possibility and he is certainly always ready to exploit it. This is precisely the area where many people feel uneasy; they are quite ready to admit in a general sense the existence of evil powers but find it difficult to grasp the reality of their actual involvement in human affairs.

This is the whole point, I believe, of the multitude of references in the book to the powers of death and chaos which are haunting Job. And this in effect means that, since the Friends cannot attribute evil and suffering to God, they are obliged to argue that Job has brought it on himself. Jesus warns against this when he heals a blind man and his disciples ask, "who sinned, this man or his parents, that he was born blind?" (John 9:2). Jesus points out that neither is the case. Not that the man was sinless, but that this blindness was not the consequence of a particular evil in that family.

In a sense, of course, what is said about the attack on Job by demonic powers must be provisional. The Old Testament cannot have a final answer to this battle with the powers of evil. We wait for the Cross and Resurrection to deal the death blow to the principalities and powers, and beyond that to the return of Christ and their final banishment. But Job has become a grand battle-ground between the forces of good and evil, and the whole universe has become a kind of background to that battle.

The Friends fail here as counsellors because they look only at the superficial; they do not get alongside Job and they misunderstand the God they profess to represent. But there is help here for anyone struggling like Job. God loves, God cares even if the opposite seems to be true. We need not be afraid to bring our hurt and anger to him. We do not have to pretend we are rejoicing and feeling good or be in any way dishonest. God understands and cares.

In a later chapter of this book we shall explore further how Christ's victory over Satan gives us a solid foundation for bringing healing into Job-like situations.

4

If It Is Not He Then Who Is It?

Job 9

At a significant point in *The Lion, the Witch and the Wardrobe*, we read this, "As Susan heard the strange name, Aslan, she began to tremble, "Oh," said Susan, "Is he quite safe?" "Safe" said Mr. Beaver, "Course he isn't safe. But he's good. He's the king I tell you."

And that brings us straight to the heart of Job 9. The 'safe' God of chapters 1 and 2 has disappeared, the sunny certainties with which the book began have vanished and there is a big question which now has to be asked, 'is he good?'. Two observations will help us to focus this.

The first is that in chapter 9 we are facing up to the very heart of what the book is about, which is not just the particular situation and troubles of Job but the very nature of God, the mystery and enigma of many of his actions. The chapter is one of tremendous literary beauty and this comes partly from a combination of two types of language. On the one hand there is hymn-like language: verse 4ff with their evocation of the majesty of wind, mountains and the starry heavens which recalls the language of the Psalter. On the other hand there is the language of the law court. Job is demanding an audience with God; he wants to appear in God's court, to present his case and have himself declared innocent. Verbs such as "answered" (Job 9:1); "contend" (Job 9:3); and "appeal" (Job 9:15) have distinct legal nuances in Hebrew which we can miss in English translations. So the big question is, how can we approach a God like this, and when we have approached him what kind of response will we get?

The second thing to notice is that Job has moved a long way from Job 3. There he was sunk in the depths of nihilism and despair; he was in a trap he could not break, a pit he could not climb out of. In the discussion of that chapter it was noted that while the answer did not come there, hints could be discerned of a possible way out: first the conviction that God is behind everything and second the total honesty with which Job spoke.

But here Job is determined to fight back. He is no longer in the stupefied state where he feels it does not matter and that nothing again will ever matter. He is not going to lie down and take it. He is going to fight back, like Abraham arguing with God to spare Sodom in Genesis 18; like Jacob wrestling with God in Genesis 32.

And Job is asking questions. If we were to be so rash as to select a text which sums up the whole book of Job, 9:24 would come as close to that as any: "if it is not he, who then is it?". In this verse Job is actually brushing against the solution to his problem. If it is not God who is responsible for all these calamities, then it is possible there may be some sinister force, a power that can imitate God so cleverly and so subtly as to appear like him.

Thus Job is wrestling with the question of God's goodness and whether other powers are at work. We shall examine how this chapter explores these questions in three spheres. First in the created order; second in society and third in his own personal life.

God in Creation (verses 1-13)

Coming first to creation we notice that Job is not the first person to speak of the created order, Eliphaz and Bildad have already done so and Zophar is about to. But the Friends, as already noted, have a totally inadequate idea of God and his creation. In particular, there are two aspects of Job's attitude to God and creation which ought to be noted.

There is first a sense of wonder and awe. In the powerful passage verse 3ff. Job creates images of tremendous impact and majesty. God's greatness is seen in earthquakes and shines from the great constellations in heaven. This sense of wonder is something which is lacking in the speeches of the Friends. But it is also significant, and this will be looked at in the discussion of chapter 38, that sometimes God appears to be echoing Job's words by, for example, mentioning the same constellations alluded to here.

Job is realizing that the solution to his problems does not just lie in himself, there are bigger and profounder issues involved. And this sense of the wonder and vastness of the universe is an integral part of a true relationship with God. Job, although hurt and angry is using the language of praise and by using that language he is showing a hunger for God. He still clings to the fact that God is behind everything. The language here recalls Psalm 46:2, "We will not fear though the earth gives way, though the mountains be moved into the heart of the sea." What matters ultimately is not changing circumstances, however alarming, but the greatness and majesty of the Creator.

The second noteworthy feature of Job's response to creation is his sense of its order. Indeed behind all response to disaster whether personal or cosmic, is this desire for order, what the Hebrews called *shalom*, which means more than peace and has nuances of harmony and wholeness. This sense of order is given classic expression in Genesis 1 with its description of the days of creation, the light spreading throughout the darkness and the gradual appearance of life in its multitude of forms. Just as in the cosmos there are tidal waves, earthquakes and great catastrophes on a communal and individual scale, so in human life there are social and personal convulsions.

But in this chapter, the sense of harmony and the threats to it are referred to in what can be described as 'mythical' language, which is to become increasingly important in the book. The particular reference is Job 9:13, "God will not turn back his anger, beneath him bowed the helpers of Rahab." This is one of the many passages in the Old Testament, especially in the poetic books where God's creating activity is expressed in terms of the defeat of the ancient powers of chaos. These powers are associated with the raging ocean and are sometimes personified under the names of Rahab or Leviathan.

A number of issues arise here. Why do the biblical writers use mythical language? What do we mean by myth? Did the biblical writers actually believe in these ancient myths? There is a very helpful discussion of these issues in C. S. Lewis' essay *Myth Become Fact*; he is not talking specifically about the book of Job, but much of what he says is relevant to the questions raised here. Lewis argues that ancient myths are 'good dreams' sent by God to prepare the world for the coming of the gospel. The gospel is like wakening up out of sleep to the daylight, but during sleep these myths are dreams, and in these myths are glimpses of the truth. They are not the full light which comes in Christ, but they are partial lights. He refers to John 1:9, "The true light, which gives light to everyone, was coming into the world", and argues, as some of the Church Fathers did, that this means that the pre-incarnate Christ enlightened the whole world in different ways and to different degrees. Lewis goes on to insist that if we are really to grasp and to be grasped by the gospel we must use our imagination as well as our mind.

Thus the Bible writers are using these images, these pictures from ancient myths to convey profound truths about the gospel. Myth is an attempt to embody great ideas in pictorial language. When we use terms such as 'light' and 'darkness' not simply to refer to physical phenomena but to spiritual life and spiritual death we are halfway to myth.

In the ancient world there were a number of myths about light and darkness being embodied in various figures who battled with each other. In particular, among Israel's neighbours there were stories of how the gods of light, order and harmony defeated the ancient gods of darkness and chaos. It seems to me that the biblical writers are using this kind of language to suggest not that the old myths, in the form which they appear, are true, but that they contain within themselves profound truth: that there is a great struggle at the very heart of creation between light and darkness.

In this sense, *The Lion, the Witch and the Wardrobe* is a modern myth. If we ask 'Is there a lion called Aslan?' Is there a personality called the White Witch?'; in one sense the answer is 'no.' Yet in another sense the dramatic story gives us a greater appreciation of the power and depth of the gospel as it fires our imagination and warms our heart.

So the language of the poet's time, alluding to stories well known helps to convey the reality of the great battle which lies at the heart of creation in which Job has been caught up. Job realizes that his tragedies are supernatural in origin. What he has yet to learn is how God is able to use these powers in his overall purpose. This, incidentally receives fascinating confirmation from modern physics which speaks of 'Chaos theory' and argues that in the whole of the creative process, chaos can form an integral part. Such is the creating power of God that even chaos serves his ultimate goal.

On a spiritual level the Old Testament is saying that the ancient power of chaos, Satan himself is ultimately as Luther called him, "God's devil" and that in the last analysis even he will have to do God's will. Paul says this explicitly in Romans 8:28, "All things (presumably including persecution, peril, sword, principalities and powers, death itself) work together for good." Paul is not saying that everything is in itself good. What he says is that in God's loving purposes all these things ultimately result in goodness, and it is a dim awareness of this that Job is showing in his sense of the order of creation. So then Job has this sense of wonder, this sense of order, and he dimly glimpses that behind the awful things happening to him lurk the powers of evil, but behind them stands the God of chapters 1 and 2.

God and Society (verses 14-24)

With that in mind we now look at the second part of the chapter which shows Job's concern for society. This comes out particularly in 9:22, "It is all one; therefore I say He destroys both the blameless and the wicked." This is developed in the following two verses in more specific ways. Even in his agony Job is not self-centred. He is in the depths of despair, sitting on an ash-heap, his family gone, his health ruined, his prospects blighted; and even in these circumstances he still has what we would call a social conscience. He still cares deeply for others and the state of society.

It is worth noting first of all his sense of justice. Just as *shalom* is vital for the cosmos, it is vital in human societies. The order of the cosmos is to be reflected in the order of society. That is classic 'Wisdom' teaching as it is presented especially in the book of Proverbs. If Satan is causing chaos in creation, then that chaos will be reflected in society as well. The whole of the cosmos, including the human part, will be affected and the natural tendency will be to place this at God's door. This is illustrated by a most poignant story.

A man was on his way to hospital to visit his little daughter who was dying of cancer. He was taking her a cake because it was her birthday, and on the way he stopped to go into a church and pray. He prayed very hard before the altar that God would spare his daughter's life. When he got to the hospital he found that his child died a few minutes earlier. If he had not stopped to pray he would have been with her when she died. He did not say, "The Lord gave and the Lord has taken away, blessed be the name of the Lord." He rushed back to the church and flung the cake at the crucifix on the altar. Who can blame him? That was an outpouring of scalding agony. And this is what Job is feeling and why he is demanding that God should explain himself. And, of course, the whole point of the book is that God is big enough to take it. Job's Friends, however, are not big enough to take it. Their God is not big enough to take it either and they think that they have to protect him against that kind of anger. The capacity to be outraged is one of the signs of a sense of justice and fairness.

The second aspect of Job's concern for society is his own example. This is implied here and is developed particularly clearly in chapter 29 which gives a moving and vivid picture of Job's life as it would have been at the beginning of chapter 1 before all these calamities happened. Not only is there a picture of the respect and affection in which he was held but a clear demonstration is given of his concern for the poor and disadvantaged, the widows and fatherless. In the Old Testament righteousness always has a social dimension and covenant is always seen in terms of community. This is clearly seen, for example in Amos and in the opening chapters of Isaiah. Being righteous always includes caring for the ills of society.

Job exemplifies this and the interesting thing is that God never disputes this at any point, and thus we have no reason to believe that Job is telling anything other than the truth. He builds up a picture of personal integrity and social justice which is very much the kind of thing commended to us in the letter of James; and, of course, James actually mentions the "steadfastness of Job" (James 5:11) as one of his examples of righteousness.

God and Job (verses 25-34)

We now come to the third part of the chapter which is how all this relates to Job himself. In these last verses, Job has an uneasy combination of, on the one hand, a longing to meet God and, on the other, extreme terror at the prospect, just as Susan in Narnia was both afraid of encountering Aslan and yet desperate to meet him.

It is important to notice Job's sense of innocence. This is perfectly genuine and we must remember that nowhere does God accuse Job of secret sin. Job's fear is not that he is guilty but that even his goodness will not help him in any kind of way that matters before God. Even human goodness will not grant him a satisfactory hearing.

There is also a sense of transience. This is brilliantly encapsulated in three images of increasing speed: a swift runner (Job 9:25); a papyrus boat skimming across the water (Job 9:26a); an eagle swooping on its prey (Job 9:26b). A similar scene is evoked in a famous passage in Bede's *Ecclesiastical History* where a missionary speaks at the court of King Edwin of Northumberland. The life of humans is compared to a sparrow that flies into the lighted hall and lingers for a moment in the warmth and then flies out again into the darkness beyond. This is basic to the human condition, the sense of the swift and inexorable passage of time.

Finally there is Job's longing for an arbiter, which we shall explore further in the next chapter, "There is no arbiter between us, who might lay his hand on us both".[1] This is a leap of faith which occurs again in chapter 16 and 19. Here the identity of the arbiter is not specified, yet the faint hope has been kindled in Job's heart that there might be someone in the heavenly court who will stand up and speak for him.

I think that in this dim shadowy figure we have one of the Old Testament intimations of the Advocate in heaven, the Advocate who is both one with God and one of us, the Advocate who is going to put his hand on us both. That is why it is so important to have a correct understanding of who Jesus is. He is not the ideal specimen of humanity standing at the head of us, to whose coat tails we hang, as it were while he stretches out his hand to touch God. Rather Jesus is the hand of God stretching out across the gulf to raise us to his presence. And this individual on the ash heap in bitter anguish and desperate agony, glimpses the heart of the gospel, an Advocate who can lay his hand on both him and God.

---

1   "There is no" could also be translated "if only there were".

5

To Whom Can We Turn?

Job 19

A friend was on a walking holiday on the island of Skye with a friend of his who is an atheist, and my friend who is a Christian, said, 'When you are a Christian, everything is different, you just step out in faith and God looks after you.' Well he stepped out in faith and landed up to his middle in a peat bog!

Job, by this stage in the book, is up to his neck, not in a peat bog but in a pit of depression and he is sorely in need of a helping hand. He is desperately longing for what is called here in chapter 19 a "redeemer." The Hebrew word is *go'el* which is difficult to represent by one English word and contains nuances of 'saviour', 'advocate' and much else.

This passage has, of course, been immortalized by Handel's music. At root is the question which Job has been asking with increasing intensity, 'how can we have a relationship with a God who causes the innocent and the good to suffer?' Now this is not a question to which there is a slick and easy answer, some convenient phrase which will make everything all right. These questions have to be wrestled with intellectually, emotionally and spiritually.

Job, in his battling with these questions, has moved on from where he was in chapter 9. There is an increasing desperation in what he says and an increasing vindictiveness in what the Friends say. In earlier speeches the Friends tended to talk in generalisations, rather vague statements about the good and the bad. Now they have become more specific and hurtful. We shall explore this further in the next chapter but look at one example here. In chapter 18, Bildad presents a grisly and gruesome picture of the fate of the wicked. Since, according to Bildad, the good do not suffer but the wicked do, Job must belong to the wicked. Job, therefore, feels that he needs to be vindicated; the longing for an advocate is becoming more desperate than ever. Indeed, he wants to have a permanent record of his thoughts and feelings, "Oh that my words were written! Oh that they were inscribed in a book! Oh that with an iron pen and lead they were engraved in the rock forever!" (Job 19:23-24).

Three questions need to be addressed. First, why particularly at this point does Job need a mediator? Second, who is that mediator? Third, what will be the result of the mediator's activities?

Why at This Point Does Job Need a Mediator?

In one sense the answer is obvious; he needs a mediator because he is harassed and persecuted beyond endurance. But there are two factors which make the need particularly at this point.

The first is that Job is *increasingly conscious that God is attacking him*. In chapter 16, Job speaks of this in extremely vivid and startling language, "I was at ease and he broke me apart, he seized me by the neck and dashed me to pieces" (Job 16:12). And yet, as we shall see, this very sense of being attacked by God is the reverse side of Job's desperate need for God. It is all so hurtful because he needs God badly and loves him deeply.

More especially, the recent chapters have been dominated by death, culminating in Job 18:14 with Bildad's grisly picture of "the king of terrors." And it is this area which raises the problem most acutely: what if Job dies unvindicated? What if he goes to his grave with his name denigrated and with nothing to show that God cares?

Job, in this chapter, describes God's attacks on him in a series of vivid pictures (Job 19:7-12). He is an individual alone and assaulted; somebody mugged in a city and calling for help while people pass by unheeding. Then he thinks of a traveller on a blocked road as night falls. There are also pictures of buildings destroyed and trees uprooted. Most devastating of all is the image of Job in his pathetic little tent, being besieged by God's enormous armies. God is attacking him and he needs to be defended.

The second element is *his sense of alienation from others which he sees as God's fault*, "He has put my brothers far from me, and those who know me are wholly estranged from me" (Job 19:13). God is not only attacking Job directly, but has turned everyone against him. This is often a painful fact of our experience; we feel that everyone has abandoned us, that nobody cares and that God himself has become hostile.

There is a good illustration of this in Mark 5. Jairus, a synagogue ruler, goes to Jesus in great distress and says, "My little girl is critically ill, will you come and help her?" Instead of helping immediately, Jesus stops to help someone else whose need is apparently less great, and during that delay Jairus' world crashes about his ears, "Jairus, don't bother the Teacher any more, she's dead." At this point Jairus must have felt that even Jesus didn't care. It is to this desperate man that Jesus responds with words which are simple but strangely powerful, "Don't be afraid, trust me." Such is the assurance that Jairus must hang on to in that dark moment. Job too is desperately searching for someone he can trust.

Who Is the Mediator?

We must remind ourselves of the basic situation of the book of Job. Job is not suffering because of a series of accidents. These events have their origin in the heavenly court and have been orchestrated by God himself. We noticed how Job had in fact glimpsed this, "If it is not he (God) then who is it?" (Job 9:24). In that same chapter (Job 9:32-35) he had spoken of an arbiter.

At that point this figure is shadowy and undefined but once this hope is expressed it cannot simply be left at that but has to be taken up and explored. In a very real sense that is true of the whole of the Old Testament. Once the offspring of the woman is mentioned in Genesis 3:15 an increasing longing is expressed for someone in whom all God's purposes will be embodied, "God's presence and his very self."[1] This hope becomes clearer in 16:19 where Job says, "Even now, behold, my witness is in heaven, and

---

1   From the hymn, "Praise to the holiest in the height" by J. H. Newman.

he who testifies for me is on high." In a leap of faith, Job almost has a vision of the heavenly court, and he catches a glimpse of someone who can put his case for him.

Job, here, I think, is glimpsing the greatest paradox of the Christian faith, whereby it almost appears to us as if there are two Gods – a God of judgment and a God of love. This is often what our experience seems to demonstrate. Sometimes God shows such love towards us that we wonder why we ever doubt him; at other times he seems to turn on us with such flinty hostility that we wonder why we ever trust him. In these latter situations God's enemy is masquerading as God and making it appear that God is the attacker. Job is terrified by this God who is hurting him so badly, but even in his hurt he remembers the good and kindly God of chapters 1 and 2 and strives to understand the paradox.

Who then is this *go'el*? In the Old Testament the word is used of God as champion of the oppressed and as kin to Israel. Sometimes the word has been rendered as 'kinsman-redeemer.' God, in other words is more than Israel's redeemer, he stands in a specific relationship to them. In Numbers 35 we read of the *go'el* of blood, sometimes called the 'avenger of blood' whose duty it was to seek out and kill someone who had murdered a member of his family.

Indeed in ancient Judaism, many of the matters which are now dealt with by the courts were handled within the family. Everything to do with marriage, for example, was a matter for the head of the family. The best example of this is the book of Ruth, where Boaz not only protects Ruth but actually marries her. The *go'el* was far more than an advocate in the legal sense, he was someone who was in an organic relationship to those he helped. The verbal form of *go'el* is often used of God rescuing his people from Egypt and from other oppressors. In many ways it is close to the word *parakleitos* in the New Testament which refers to the Holy Spirit and emphasizes relationship as well as representation.

Is this *go'el*, then, God himself. Many commentators argue that it cannot possibly be God because God is the judge. How can the judge also be the defence counsel? Normally, of course, that would be impossible, but that is to misunderstand the thrust of the book. If it is God who is being accused of being the attacker, and if a *go'el* is someone who represents the weak and helpless against the strong, then who but God can negotiate with God?

What Will Be the Result of the Mediator's Activities?

Granted that Job needs a *go'el* because of God's perceived hostility, and granted that the *go'el* can be none other than God himself, what will happen. Two matters are worth noting.

First of all, this *go'el* will "stand upon the earth" (Job 19:25) or literally 'stand upon the dust.' The 'dust', especially in poetry, can refer to the grave and the world beyond. Is this a glimpse of life beyond death? The letter to the Hebrews speaks of this in relation to Abraham and others who are looking for a city whose builder and architect is God (Hebrews 11:10). The writer goes on to say that they were looking for a better country, a heavenly one (Hebrews 11:16). Is Job here catching a glimpse of the promised land?

To talk of heaven is to risk being labelled 'other-wordly' and to be the butt of snide remarks: 'too heavenly-minded to be of any earthly use'— not that I have ever met anyone in my life like that. But the point is that heaven is not an optional extra, heaven is the unveiled presence of God. And it seems that what has happened for a moment is that the world beyond has broken into Job's world. Surrounded as he is by negative images, the life of the world to come has shone briefly into his darkness. Charles Wesley speaks of this in one of his greatest hymns, "I woke, the dungeon flamed with light."[2]

Job's dungeon does not exactly flame with light, but a ray of light has penetrated, a key has clanked in the door; there is hope, there is dawn beyond the night. As already noted, 'dust' can mean the grave. Is this a picture of the *go'el* trampling underfoot the power of death? Obviously such an idea awaits the Resurrection and the Empty Tomb for its full meaning, yet this is one of the Old Testament's glimpses of the final victory over death and the power of the grave. In this moment of agony Job glimpses beyond this world and this life to someone who will stand on the dust and trample underfoot all the negative and hostile powers which are ranged against him.

The second prominent note in this passage is the emphasis on 'seeing' God. Job says "in my flesh I shall see God, whom I shall see for myself, and my eyes behold and not another" (Job 19:26-27). Many commentators argue that this means he expects his vindication to come while he is still alive in this world. That is true in itself because Job says, "I had heard of you by the hearing of the ear, but now my eyes see you." (Job 42:5). However, the

2   From the hymn, "*And can it be?*" by Charles Wesley.

phrase "in my flesh" implying while I am still in this world could equally be translated 'from' or 'out of' my flesh, suggesting after I have left this world. In a real sense this does not matter, the important thing is not when and where he sees God but that he will see God. And that is what Christian living is about. In the book of Revelation, where in image after image the new creation has been summoned up, a phrase in the final chapter crystallises it all, "His servants will worship him. They will see his face." (Revelation 22:3-4).

This is wonderfully expressed in a passage towards the end of *The Screwtape Letters* where Screwtape writes to Wormwood in baffled rage at how at the moment of death their 'patient' had entered the life everlasting.

> "One moment it seemed to be all our world, the
> scream of bombs, the fall of houses, the stink and taste
> of high explosive on the lips and in the lungs; the feet
> burning with weariness, the heart cold with horrors,
> the legs aching, the brain reeling. Next moment
> all this was gone: gone like a bad dream. Defeated,
> outmanoeuvred fool, did you mark how naturally the
> earth-born vermin entered the new life?"

Then this:

> "He saw him. This animal, this thing begotten in a bed,
> could look on him. What is blinding, suffocating fire
> to you is now cool light to him, is clarity itself and
> wears the form of a man."

"He saw him", that is the ultimate answer to Job's and to all our tragedies.

6

Not Speaking What Is Right

Job 15-25

The title for this chapter comes from Job 42:7 where God gives his assessment of what the Friends have said. In a previous chapter of this book, we looked at their contributions in the early part of the dialogue. Here we shall examine their later contributions which are marked by increasing bitterness and condemnation.

Eliphaz's speech in chapter 15 is full of cynical condemnation and dismisses Job's words as "windy knowledge" and "the tongue of the crafty." Ironically in 15:8 he accuses Job of pretending to "have listened in the council of God." As we have seen Job does have some conception of the divine council in contrast to Eliphaz and the others who appear to have no such knowledge. He continues by outlining the fate of "the wicked man" (Job 15:20) and "the godless" (Job 15:34) by whom he means Job.

He gives Job no consolation, only warning that he will suffer retribution. In his world there is no place for honest questioning of God, only punishment and darkness await Job. To Eliphaz,

Job must repent of his sins otherwise there is no hope for him at all.

If Eliphaz has left Job completely without hope Bildad speaks with grisly relish of the death which awaits the wicked (Job 18). There is no attempt to dialogue with Job and no praise of God. There is not a shred of sympathy for Job's suffering, indeed a worse fate awaits him at the hands of "the king of terrors" (Job 18:14).

Zophar in chapter 20 completes the denunciation with a tirade on the fate of the evildoer and it is very plain that he is interpreting Job's calamities as deserved punishment for his sins (Job 20:28-29). There is no hint that this can be avoided and no call to repentance. Zophar has made up his mind and has nothing else to say.

Bildad's final contribution in chapter 25 is short and some have argued that his words continue in chapter 26. However, the contrast between the two chapters is stark and the supposed similarities relate to subject matter. Indeed 25:1-3 sound like part of a hymn of praise but 25:4-6 disparage the created order and fail to see humanity as God's image. Indeed Bildad scans the universe and sees only the reflection of his sour face and judgmental attitude. God pronounced his creation "good"; Bildad apparently knows better.

Totally absent from chapter 25 (and the other chapters from the Friends) is the sense of wonder and awe at the majesty of God. They pay lip service to the wonder of the Creator and his creation but have no sense of worship; rather their comments are cold and lacking any depth and a realization of their own sinfulness.

Also there is no sense of mystery in what they say. In their mechanical universe Job must be a great sinner because he is suffering so much. It is important to see exactly what God says in 42:7, "You have not spoken *of me* what is right."[1] The words "*of me*" are the most significant part of the phrase. They may have said many things which are right in themselves, but since they have misrepresented God that ultimately means that all that they say is fatally flawed. Their God is too small and the true God cannot be confined in their narrow thinking. Indeed the supreme irony is that the man they believe to be condemned is the one whose prayers will be accepted and save them from the consequences of their folly.

One obvious question is why do we have so much from the Friends, given that what they say is at best misleading? We need to see this as an important part of establishing the truth. Just as the prophets tell us the false teaching of those who mislead, as do the apostles, so that we can recognize error when we encounter it, so here the truth is established by showing what is false.

Speaking of God is never something to be undertaken lightly and needs true humility and a realization that we can never know all there is to be known. The Friends lack any sense that they do not know everything and thus there is a frightening lack of humility and empathy in what they say.

1   Emphasis mine.

7

Where Can Wisdom Be Found?

Job 28

There can be no doubt that Job has travelled a long way since the agonies of chapter 3, and that the *go'el* passage in chapter 19 has marked a significant breakthrough, an enormous leap of faith in the darkness. Much ground has still to be travelled, though, and there is to be no immediate easing of Job's situation. Indeed, as we have seen, the immediate response to Job's speech is a particularly vindictive tirade by Zophar which includes a grisly description of how the wicked will meet their fate. This is followed by a more measured, but no less condemnatory speech by Eliphaz in chapter 22, which is a legal indictment of Job as a wicked man and a summons to him to repent.

To these Job replies in chapters 23-24 with an impassioned appeal for a hearing in the heavenly court, including an eloquent plea for justice for the poor and needy. Many have argued that these words, particularly 24:18-25, cannot be by Job because they appear to be diametrically opposed to his claim in chapter 21 that the innocent suffer and the guilty prosper. Chapter 24 claims, as the Friends do, that punishment for the wicked is inevitable and inexorable. But Job has never disputed that God will judge the wicked, what he has maintained is that he is not one of them. This is the thrust of 24:25, "If it is not so, who will prove me a liar and show there is nothing in what I say." There is no need to attribute this part of the speech to Zophar or Bildad.

That illustrates a wider problem of this whole section of the book which contains the majestic poem to Wisdom in chapter 28, our main subject in this chapter. What is the relation of this poem to chapters 24-31? What is its purpose in the flow of the book, especially in relation to God's speeches in chapters 38-41? We shall first of all explore the context, then look at the development of the chapter itself, and finally reflect on the issues raised by this presentation of wisdom.

We have plainly reached a stage in the book of Job where the debate is running into trouble and the reader is wondering if the gigantic problems raised are going to be solved. Chapter 28 appears out of place with its calm and measured tone, compared with the frenetic speeches surrounding it. The text as it stands appears to regard the chapter as part of a speech by Job, and yet chapters 26-31 seems inordinately long for such a speech, and the lack of speeches of reply by the Friends, except for the inordinately brief speech of Bildad in chapter 25, have led many commentators to reassign and rearrange these chapters. My argument is that chapters 26-31 have an essentially choric function and bring together much of the theology and imagery of the earlier chapters, thus providing a secure basis for the divine speeches where all these matters are definitively addressed.

It may also be, as already noticed that the Friends have run out of things to say. Zophar sputters out in angry silence in chapter 20, and Job turns his words against him (Job 27:13–23). Similarly, Eliphaz, in chapter 22, gives a legalistic indictment (much of which Job answers in chapters 29-31) where what Job says sounds like the final summing up of a defence counsel. Bildad peters out in sour and patronizing commonplaces (see chapter 25) very different from the magnificent words of Job in chapter 26.

Thus what we are given now is an overview of the imagery and themes of the book which both summarises the journey already travelled and points forward to the next stage. Chapter 26 encapsulates the wonders and mysteries of creation and cosmic evil. Indeed this can be seen as another of Job's leaps of faith, because the structure of what he says anticipates the thrust of God's own speeches in chapters 38-41. 26:1-4 are a challenge, which God takes up in chapter 38 as he begins to speak; 26:5-10 correspond to the rest of chapters 38-39 where God evokes the mysteries of the universe. 26:11-14 refer to the mysteries of supernatural evil which is the thrust of chapters 40-41. Thus Job is showing that openness to God which is at the heart of any true relationship with him.

Chapter 27 turns to legal imagery and the court scene with the adversary, a vivid reminder of chapters 1-2. Job's reference to the "ways" of God in 26:14 have reminded him forcefully of the mystery of divine providence and his inability to explain these ways. Job uses the words of the Friends against them and shows the human as well as the cosmic side of tragedy as he speaks of starving children, destitute widows and loss of home and possessions.

Leaving chapter 28 aside for a moment, we glance at chapters 29-31 which are Job's final summing up of the case for his innocence. Chapter 29 paints a vivid picture of a peaceful and harmonious society which reflects the ordered government of the universe unfolded in chapter 28. Chapter 30, by contrast, shows images of deprivation and terror and thus draws on the dark side of the mystery of God's ways in creation. Moreover, like chapter 3, it contains images of 'uncreation,' e.g. light turning to darkness (Job 30:26). Chapter 31 represents the culmination of legal language in the speech cycles with Job's protestations of innocence and purity. The emphasis is on inner attitudes rather than outward actions. Job in these closing words is arguing that he is in tune with the Creator's purpose and thus his case deserves an answer.

It is in this context that we examine chapter 28 and its exploration of the theme of Wisdom. The chapter can conveniently be divided into three parts: 28:1-11 the difficult search for wisdom; 28:12-22 the inaccessibility of wisdom; 28:23-28 wisdom and creation. Since the chapter is a kind of pause for reflection we shall not be surprised to find many echoes of the journey thus far as well as anticipations of what is to come.

The search for wisdom (Job 28:1-11) draws on the dangers of mining to illustrate the formidable difficulties in the quest. The vivid and tangible nature of the description reminds us that the sorrows of Job had not only been in his mind but had been very real and palpable. He had been in the blackest darkness and assailed by a crushing sense of isolation.

A second feature of this section is the theme of intense probing and searching; wisdom will not yield her secrets easily.

This is underlined by the commodities mentioned in verses 5-6: bread with all the process of sowing, reaping and the sustaining of life; and precious stones with suggestions of costly effort. Searching for wisdom will be no less costly.

Mere human wisdom and achievement are not condemned, any more than Job's wealth and happiness were condemned in the Prologue. Verse 1, about the refining of gold, plainly echoes 23:10, "when he has tested me, I shall come out as gold." The picture of mining reflects Job's search for the Divine wisdom which lies behind creation.

The question implied in comparing the search for wisdom to mining is now addressed in the second section (Job 28:12-22) on the inaccessibility of wisdom. The key words 'wisdom' and 'understanding' are taken up by God in chapters 38-39 and put into proper perspective. This chapter is an anticipation of that and a powerful reminder that all human searching and exploring is futile without God's revelation. Verses 13-14 state that wisdom cannot be found by ransacking the human and material universe. We may find glimpses of it but wisdom itself still eludes us. We are being prepared for the awesomeness of God's own speeches and the proper humility of realising our own smallness in the scheme of things.

Wisdom, like love in the Song of Songs 8:7, cannot be bought. The richest treasures of the exotic east are weighed in the balance against wisdom and found wanting. We are being forced gradually into a recognition of the severe limits of human power and understanding. Even in the realms beyond human understanding — pathless heavens and the realms of destruction and death — only very faint rumours of wisdom can be found.

In the final section (Job 28:23-28) it is interesting to note that wisdom is scarcely mentioned, rather it is God's power in creation which is celebrated. He knows and understands because he is the Creator and his seeing is part of his creating activity (see in Genesis 1). True seeing by mortals is thus a gift from God and requires his revelation of himself. This is exactly what God is shortly to do for Job as he takes him on a tour of the wonders of the universe.

The details of creation in verses 25-26 are full of interest. The poet selects phenomena — wind, rain, lightning and thunder — which are generally seen as the most elusive and unpredictable and shows how they are governed by fixed patterns, "when he made a decree for the rain and a way for the lightning of the thunder." Moreover, these represent the forces of nature which are ambiguous and can be both lifegiving and destructive, which exactly demonstrates the riddle about the ways of God which is at the heart of the book.

This section is summed up in verses 27-28. Verse 27 is a general statement about creation and the wisdom which lies at its heart. The full implications of this verse are still to be explored in chapters 38-41. Once again the importance of 'seeing' is underlined reminding us of 19:26-27, "in my flesh I shall see God, whom I shall see for myself, and my eyes shall behold", and pointing forward to 42:5, "I had heard of you by the hearing of the ear, but now my eye sees you".

In Genesis 1, God looks on his creation and pronounces it 'good', and in Job God's seeing includes 'confirming' and 'testing', words which have implications of probing and exploring; God is telling Job that there are depths and mysteries in the universe of which he knows nothing.

Verse 28 stands somewhat apart from the poem with its introductory phrase "and he said to man". This is a reminder that the book is wider than the specific situation of Job himself. Wisdom cannot be found by the most rigorous search yet there is a way to experience it. That way is the 'fear of the LORD' exemplified by Job in chapter 1.

We are now in a position to reflect on the issues raised by this chapter at this point in the book. The journey we have travelled has mirrored much of human experience as it wrestles with the mysteries of living and dying. Chapters 1-2 give us the story on its different levels: the rapid unfolding of the catastrophes which reduce Job's world to dust and ashes and the orchestration of these events in the heavenly court. This emphasized the need for vision to penetrate beyond the outward events. Then followed the numb despair of chapter 3 and the inadequacy of the Friends as counsellors. The dialogue develops with its blend of angry protest, misunderstandings, claims and counterclaims. This is a necessary journey to travel: the dark night must be lived through, the hard questions asked, the great issues grappled with.

Chapter 28 is thus a vital pause and, with its calm and measured tone, it invites reflection. The themes and images of the chapter are brilliantly used to further the flow of the book. The description of mining not only suggests suffering and solitude which mirrors Job's plight, but also evokes the mysteries of the underworld. Moreover, there is a profound admiration of human ingenuity which is in contrast to Bildad's sour dismissal of humans as "maggots" (Job 25:6); yet we are also shown human limitations; with all our powers we are unable to find wisdom.

The 'debate', however, has ground to a halt with the Friends becoming ever more condemnatory, and while Job has shown astonishing insights at some points,[1] chapter 27 has shown that his insight has proved ineffective as a bulwark against depression. Thus, here in chapter 28, a statement of the fundamental wisdom and order underlying the universe is necessary and allows a breathing space for passions to subside. Job's long speech (chapters 29-31) is a final summing-up for the defence in which he gives his reasons for claiming that he has in fact walked in 'the fear of the LORD'.

Three comments conclude our consideration of chapter 28. The first is that this chapter is a theological consideration of the place of wisdom in creation and one which ranges from the depths of the earth to the furthest reaches of sea and sky. Theology is necessary; we must think large thoughts about God, creation and humanity. Yet theology is not enough (we shall explore this further in our consideration of the Elihu speech), and only hearing and seeing God will address the huge issues raised in the book. Theology, properly used, is an important step along that way.

Secondly, this chapter has a realistic view of human potential and limitations. The view of humanity which emerges is firmly in line with Old Testament teaching. In Genesis 1:26-27 where the creation of humans occurs, the word *ba'ra* (to create) only ever used of God in the Bible, is used three times, having been sparingly employed in the previous verses. Yet humans are

---

1   For example, chapters 9 and 19.

not the whole of creation, they are given only part of Day 6. Similarly, in Psalm 8 humans appear insignificant under the awesome beauty of the starry heavens, yet they are "a little lower than the angels." Here in Job 28 the considerable achievements of humans are celebrated: the penetrating into the remote recesses of the earth, the wresting of its treasures from the soil and geographical and cosmological discoveries. Yet wisdom and the mysteries of creation and the control of the elements are beyond human understanding.

Finally, 'the fear of the Lord' can never simply be a matter of theory, as if grasping it by the mind meant that we now *know* what wisdom is. The parallel phrase 'to shun evil' shows that a whole way of life is involved. This has been true of Job as outlined by the narrator in chapter 1, and is to be developed by Job himself in chapters 29-31. So we are still waiting for an answer: why has this wise man been treated thus?

8

Trying to Tie Him Down

Job 32-37

Many years ago I heard an evangelistic sermon which used as its text Job 36:18. In the King James version this reads, "Because there is wrath, beware lest he take thee away with his stroke; then a great ransom cannot deliver thee". Incidentally, most of the modern versions translate it differently.[1] The sermon talked of the danger of treating God's anger lightly and failing to repent and receive forgiveness.

However, that sermon could have more appropriately been preached from a passage such as Romans 3 where such truths are explicitly taught rather than taking Elihu's words out of context and treating them as if they were authoritative theology. Elihu's words, like those of the other speakers have to be judged by God's own words in chapters 38-41, and by the final part of the story in chapter 42. Seen in this light, Elihu's contribution is found wanting. To be truly biblical in our thinking we must take books as a whole and listen to their distinctive message and

---

1   For example, in the ESV, "Beware lest wrath entice you into scoffing, and let not the greatness of the ransom turn you aside."

not simply fillet them for texts which illustrate the distinctive message of other biblical books.

It is true that Elihu says some good things and we shall look at these, but the flaw is that what he says is theoretical and lacks pastoral warmth. I have already mentioned C. S. Lewis' powerful book *A Grief Observed*, written when his wife died. Many years before this, he wrote one of his fine apologetic works *The Problem of Pain* which wrestles bravely and honestly with the mystery of suffering in a world created and sustained by a loving God. Lewis makes many valid and penetrating points in that book, but whereas the later book sprang from intense personal grief, the earlier one has the atmosphere of the study and the debating chamber. That is right and valuable in its place but is no cure for the black depression and broken heart of someone like Job. Elihu's contribution is long on theology and short on pastoral concern.

So it is that Elihu tries to tie God down and gives to Job a theology of creation and suffering which fails to address the real issues. He speaks at great length and there is a fair amount of repetition in what he says. Many commentators, indeed, have dismissed these chapters (32-37) as a later interpolation and seen them as inferior to the rest of the book. It is further pointed out that he is introduced abruptly and that, most strikingly of all, God ignores his contribution. That view, I think, misunderstands the significance of the speech. The poetry of the speech is indeed inferior to the magnificence of chapters 38-41, but surely we would expect the best poetry to be reserved for God! Moreover, the fact that God ignores him is rather a comment on the fact that he is simply to be taken as another character in the drama and not on his own terms as adjudicator and arbiter. So we shall first look at Elihu himself; then make some comments on the substance of what he says and finally reflect on the significance of these chapters in the book of Job as a whole.

Elihu Himself

Elihu is introduced by a prose prologue (Job 32:1-5) indicating a new stage of the action. As we noticed in our discussion of chapter 28 the contribution of the Friends has run into the sand and 31:40 has stated "the words of Job are ended." The Friends have failed to provide an answer and Job's conviction of his own righteousness has not been shaken. It is at this point that Elihu assumes the mantle of arbiter and proceeds to give his exposition of what he sees as the reality of the situation He has clearly listened to the dialogue and, as we shall see, there are many references and allusions to what the other characters have said. The author skilfully suggests how we are to regard Elihu's contribution by deftly pointing out features of his personality.

First of all he is presented as an angry young man. Four times we are told he is angry, not perhaps the most promising way to begin what purports to be an authoritative disclosure of the ways of God. He is also shown to be egocentric: "Therefore, I say, listen to me; let me also declare my opinion" (Job 32:10); "I also will answer with my share; I also will declare my opinion" (Job 32:17).

This cleverly underlines the difference between Elihu's self-image and the way he actually appears. There is a patronizing tone to what he says and he uses the technique of superficial respect to be scathingly dismissive and the language of modesty to disguise arrogance.

Elihu's Arguments

With this in mind, let's look at the substance of what he says. In chapters 32-33 he uses the legal language we have become so familiar with throughout the book. At first sight he appears to have a wider vision than the Friends whom he castigates for their failure to answer Job, "behold, there was none among you who refuted Job or who answered his words" (Job 32:12) but his fire is equally directed against Job. His windy rhetoric in 32:15-22 for all its high flown vocabulary amounts to the claim that Elihu is bursting to say something.

What he does say summons Job to a formal hearing in court, "Answer me, if you can; set your words in order before me; take your stand" (Job 33:5). In 33:8-11 Elihu draws from various speeches of Job (e.g. Job 9:20-21; 27:5-6; 31:6). Then he specifically turns to Job's often repeated complaint that God will not give him a hearing. After the elaborate build up we are hardly set alight by his statement (Job 33:12) that "God is greater than man", undoubtedly true but scarcely an original contribution. He then speaks of various ways in which God does speak to humans: by dreams (Job 33:15-18); by sickness (Job 33:19-23) and by healing (Job 33:24-28).

None of this can be disputed but the point of the book is that Job does not understand what God is saying to him through his sickness and other calamities. As for dreams, these have been an added burden, "you scare me with dreams and terrify me with visions" (Job 7:14). One of the important things the writer is doing in the Elihu speech is reminding us of many of the things that Job has said just before God answers them.

Chapter 34 is set in a world of courts and litigation as Elihu sets out a defence of God's government of the universe. Here he is responding to Job's questioning of God's providence in such passages as chapter 9 and 12:13-25. Elihu shows here no pastoral concern, he wants to beat Job into submission. God has absolute power and he is guiltless. This is exactly what Job acknowledges in 42:2, "I know that you can do all things, and that no purpose of yours can be thwarted". Elihu's words, however, contribute nothing to this change in Job, it is the revelation of God himself which does this. Elihu sees God's judgment as mainly punitive (Job 34:16-37), a direct attack on what Job says in 9:23-35. This has none of the compassion which marks Job's speeches, notably chapter 24.

In Chapter 35 Elihu turns to the subject of God's detachment (Job 35:5-6). God, he alleges, does not listen to human cries because those who cry are hypocrites (Job 35:12-13) Now this can be true in some cases such as Psalm 66:18, "If I had cherished iniquity in my heart, the Lord would not have listened." But this is emphatically not the case with Job. Indeed, if Elihu is right, God simply will not appear to Job at all. Elihu is right to state that God is far beyond our understanding but wrong when he reasons that God is far too great to care for humans. The right way to reason is that of Isaiah 40 where the overwhelming grandeur of God is celebrated as the reason for trusting him, "They who wait for the LORD shall renew their strength; they shall mount up with wings like eagles; they shall run and not grow weary; they shall walk and not faint" (Isaiah 40:31). Indeed Elihu's condemnation of Job, "Job opens his mouth in empty talk; he multiplies words without knowledge" (Job 35:16) could be a fair description of much of his own speech.

Finally in chapters 36-37 Elihu turns to justify the ways of God in creation and providence. He argues that God sends suffering to give people a deeper understanding of his ways. The fundamental problem in all this is that Job has never denied the unfathomable greatness of God; we noticed this especially in chapters 9 and 26. Elihu becomes eloquent as he speaks of the glories of creation and especially the power of God in clouds, storms and thunder. Indeed, as he speaks, a thunderstorm gathers, "Keep listening to the thunder of his voice and the rumbling that comes from his voice" (Job 37:2), and it is from this storm that God speaks (Job 38:1). Yet Elihu lacks the sense of his own ignorance but is perfectly convinced of Job's ignorance.

Elihu goes on to say that just as no one can look at the sun in its blazing splendour, no one can expect a private appearance of God yet it is just such an appearance which is about to happen.

What Part Does Elihu's Speech Play in the Book as a Whole?

Plainly Elihu has said some good things and has some useful insights. Yet in the overall message of the book he does not bring about the healing and comfort Job needs. So what can we learn from these chapters?

First of all there is the salutary lesson that even the speaking of truth, if it is not done from a heart of love, is more likely to lead to hurt and confusion than to transformation. Elihu takes great slabs of truth and constructs a monstrous edifice without doors or windows. Thus it is that those who want to apply the living truth to their contemporaries must do so in a spirit of humility and willingness to learn themselves. Elihu's comments are not marked by the spirit of prayer, they are the words of someone convinced he is totally right and the atmosphere is like the cold icy wind of which he speaks (Job 37:8-11).

The second thing to observe is that, although Elihu sometimes comes nearer to the truth than the Friends do, he does not grasp the most basic reality about the situation which is that Job is in no doubt about the majesty and power of God but has lost confidence in God's good intentions towards him. It is precisely in this area of relationships that the shortcomings of all four, Elihu as well as Eliphaz, Bildad and Zophar are most glaring. None of them offer to pray with Job, they are far too concerned to convince him of the rightness of what they say.

But most important of all, Elihu is ultimately wrong because God does appear. What follows in chapters 38-41 is one of the great theophanies of Scripture; comparable to Jacob wrestling with God (Genesis 32); Moses at the Burning Bush (Exodus 3); Isaiah in the Temple (Isaiah 6) and John on Patmos seeing the Risen Lord (Revelation 1). We shall examine this in the next chapters but it is worth noting at this point that it is to be God himself and not simply statements about him, who is to bring the answer.

9

The Grandeur of God

Job 38-39

In one of her meditations, Lady Julian of Norwich tells of a vision of God where He holds in his hand a small round object like a nut. When she asked what it was God replied 'Everything that is.' The universe is indeed vast and mysterious but compared to God it is tiny. The chapters we now consider (Job 38-39) indeed evoke the mysteries of the cosmos but even more the immensity of God. G. M. Hopkins speaks of this in his poem, *The Grandeur of God*, where he sees the living Spirit moving, penetrating, energizing every living thing, but also sees the treading and toiling generations and the dark mystery which lies at the heart of creation. It is this mystery which we expect God to address.

We have already looked at how the debate appears to run into the sand after chapter 24, and how further progress appears to be further impeded by Elihu's long speech (Job 33-37). Human wisdom is being given a run for its money; everyone has been allowed to speak at great length. So when God speaks at the eleventh hour it is significant that he speaks from a storm. In chapter 1 a violent storm had destroyed Job's family. In chapter 9 Job had spoken of God being active in the forces of nature at their most terrifying, in storms, earthquakes and eclipses. Thus God speaks right out of the heart of the mystery.

It is also most significant that God is given his covenant name, *Yahweh*, a name which does not occur often in the book. The poet here is making the point that this is the God who is the protector of his people, who is committed to them by promises that he cannot and will not break. This is not some remote deity living far away across leagues of space. This is Yahweh revealing himself as the *go'el* for whom Job had longed. Yet when he speaks out of the storm, rather than giving answers, he asks questions — "Who is this that darkens counsel by words without knowledge?" (Job 38:2).

In one sense that is putting Job in his place; there is much of which he is ignorant. In another sense it is meeting Job at his point of his need and proceeding to open up dimensions of the problem of which he was totally unaware. As we explore this cascade of questions there are three areas to examine: the sheer Greatness of God; the Care and Providence of God, and finally the Joy of God.

The Greatness of God

The greatness and grandeur of God shine through every word in this magnificent poem in chapters 38-39. For most of this book, the God perceived by the actors in the drama has been 'too small', to borrow the words of J. B. Phillips, the eminent Bible translator of the twentieth century. The God of the Friends has certainly been too small, trapped in a universe of cause and effect of which he is apparently the slave. Elihu has seen further but lacked a becoming humility in the face of mystery. Job himself has seen further in his leaps of faith, especially in chapter 19, and in the splendid wisdom poem of chapter 28 has established some important truths. But no-one has seen far enough. God is far greater, far vaster than anyone in the book has yet realised.

Moreover, it is not just the miracle of creation but God's continuing control of it which is emphasised. God is not only the Creator who in the beginning created the heavens and the earth, but the God who day by day continually creates and directs, "Have you ever given orders to the morning?" (Job 38:12 NIV); "Do you know when the mountain goats give birth?" (Job 39:1).

It is further noteworthy that God points out that creation does not centre around humans. This is strikingly illustrated in 38:26, "To bring rain on a land where no man is, on the desert in which there is no man." Our age tends to be people and problem centred. We tend to judge people and situations on how they will affect us. Our theology often is made up of what will make us feel good. That tends to be where we begin and we are inclined to fashion our idea of God very subjectively. That does not mean that we are unimportant to God and that our concerns are a matter of indifference to him. Indeed they are so important that we must apply the right medicine, begin at the right place, and that is not ourselves. If we begin with ourselves we will simply become more and more introspective and depressed. But God is directing Job, and us, to a wider panorama and vaster horizons. It is not, however, simply vastness which God emphasises, it is the intricate and detailed network of creation. We are taken on a mind-bending tour of the cosmos, from the depths of Sheol to the great constellations in heaven and shown wild animals in strange and exotic locations.

This leads to another aspect of the greatness of God: his awesomeness and otherness. This is the sense sometimes called numinous, the feeling we have all had, perhaps on a moonlit night, on a woodland path or in a glorious ancient building and it is wonderfully evoked in these chapters. This is the experience of God as a palpable reality when the veil is thin and his presence which is always there becomes a felt experience. When Jacob falls asleep at a place he later calls Bethel, he has a dream of angels ascending and descending a ladder and he awakes with an awesome sense of the presence of God (Genesis 28). John on Patmos sees the Risen Lord and falls down like someone dead (Revelation 1). A good example, on a popular level is to be found in *The Wind in the Willows* when Rat and Mole approach Pan on the island.

> "Rat, he found breath to whisper, are you afraid?
> Afraid, murmured Rat, his eyes shining with
> unutterable love. Afraid of him? Oh never, never. Yet,
> and yet, I am afraid."

This sheer mystery of God does far more than any refutation could do to rebuke the platitudes of the Friends. They think they have God taped, they think that they can put him in a box. God simply sets aside all they have said, and without ever actually contradicting it, simply marginalises it. This creates the kind of atmosphere in which the further revelation of chapters 40-41 and the resolution of chapter 42 are possible.

The Providence of God

Related to this is the second great theme of these chapters: the care and providence of God.

Essentially the theology of the Friends (and indeed, Elihu) has seen God as a kind of heavenly policeman, an agent of law and order, who pronounces Job guilty. Instead these chapters show, in Dante's words, *"the love that moves the sun and the other stars."*[1] At the heart of the universe is no remote, chilling, mechanical deity but the loving God of chapter 1.

This is brought out in a detailed way as God leads Job through an exploration of the mysteries of the created order. And what a vivid and memorable journey it is: the music of the spheres, the majesty of the sea, the earth's features like clay under a seal, the depths of the underworld, snow, rain, hail, lightning, the procession of the seasons and the wild and strange beauty of animal life. This is not merely for poetic effect; Job's crushed and broken spirit is beginning to be healed by the beauty and mystery of the world.

Notice what God is doing: He is making Job his confidant and companion. He is saying, 'Come Job, I'm going to take you on a tour of the universe. You have seen stars and sea and sky, you know about snow, rain, hail, horses and eagles, but you have never seen all these things in my company, you have never understood the created order from my perspective.' So God builds on Job's partial insights in earlier chapters such as 9 and 28, and by doing so leads him towards healing.

This is strikingly developed in chapter 39. This is more than a random selection of animals. Rather it is a picture of the life

---

1   Dante, *The Divine Comedy Paradiso*, Canto 33.

cycle itself. "Do you know when the mountain goats give birth?" (Job 39:1). This is the fundamental mystery of life, the moment of birth, to which, we may remember, Job had reacted negatively (Job 3:3-19). Creation goes on, birth is always a reality, new life is continually appearing.

Then in 39:5-12 we have two opposite examples of the fundamental mystery of the life cycle. There is first the mystery of freedom as the wild donkey roams the salt flats indifferent to humans; then there is the mystery of domesticity: why is it that the wild ox cannot be tamed and pressed into service?

The centre of the chapter (39:13-18) is a kind of *reductio ad absurdum*, a comic vignette of the mystery of life as we laugh with the poet at the crazy antics of the ostrich. She is cavalier about her eggs but has a compensating swiftness which allows her to escape from predators.

Then we have two pictures of death, the other end of the life cycle. In 39:19-25 the warhorse, whose own wild instincts are harnessed by men in the business of war, is vividly evoked, and the clanging consonants in the Hebrew text most effectively reinforce the vividness of the word picture. Finally in 39:26-30 we are in the savage world of birds of prey; "*nature red in tooth and claw*" to borrow Tennyson's phrase, the cruelty running through the world of nature.

Now this whole chapter dramatizes the mystery of providence and free will. These creatures like the phenomena of chapter 38 are free and untameable by humans, yet they can operate only within the limits God lays down, a point of enormous significance for the interpretation of the Behemoth and Leviathan passages (Job 40-41). Moreover, God is showing Job that this mysterious interplay of providence and free will lies at the very heart of creation and thus at the root of Job's problem. The care and providence of God is not something mechanical, it is the continuing process of his involvement with his creation.

The Joy of God

But thirdly, there is another deep melody sounding through these chapters and that is the joy of God. These chapters have the exuberance of great hymns of praise, the note which predominates in the psalms of praise and thanksgiving such as Psalm 19:1; 104:24; 148:7-8. This is especially underlined in Job 38:7, "When the morning stars sang together and all the sons of God shouted for joy." The whole of creation becomes a vast orchestra and we are invited to join in the symphony of praise.

Thus the question arises: why did Job not have an awareness of this symphony of praise in chapter 3? Why have we to wait as nearly forty chapters roll their majestic way to reach this point? But Job could not simply jump from his despairing and nihilistic grief to singing and pretending everything was all right. A chorus, once popular, asserted that '*a little talk with Jesus makes it right, all right.*' Now the book of Job shows us how hollow and superficial that is. We cannot simply jump from chapters 1-2 to chapter 42 and pretend that the journey of chapters 3-41 was unnecessary. If Job is going to join in this kind of praise he has to work through the darkness first. He has to go down to the depths of Sheol before he can re-ascend to the heavens. He has to face Leviathan and see evil unmasked.

Two observations can be made.

The first is that God uses many of the details Job himself had used earlier. It is no accident that God mentions in chapter 38 exactly the same constellations that Job had mentioned in chapter 9. But the difference is that God is revealing secrets known only to the Creator. The atmosphere is like that other great chapter of creation and providence, Isaiah 40, "He who brings out their host in number, calling them all by name; by the greatness of his might, and because he is strong in power, not one is missing." Divine providence is detailed and meticulous in care for all it has made. This remains true whatever Job's or our experience may be. Perhaps the best commentary on this is in the Psalter.

> *"Where shall I go from your Spirit?*
> *Or where shall I flee from your presence?*
> *If I ascend to heaven, you are there!*
> *If I make my bed in Sheol you are there!*
> *If I take the wings of the morning*
> *and dwell in the uttermost parts of the sea,*
> *even there your hand shall lead me,*
> *and your right hand shall hold me."* (Psalm 139:7-10)

The second thing to notice is that God himself is the answer. Ultimately this is not nature poetry, but poetry about God. Healing, in other words, is not to be found in nature. There is a kind of healing to be found there; it is a good thing to get away from stone, lime, buildings and noise, from cars, buses and trains and to go out to moorland or woodland or walk by sea and river. We all know that can do us good, make us feel better and helps us to see things in perspective.

But in situations such as those described in Job 1-2, nature will not heal us nor take away the aching sense of loss. We must avoid making extravagant claims for nature. Wordsworth, although a great and sensitive poet, sometimes does so, as in his unfortunate line, *'Nature never did betray the heart who loved her.'* Had he never heard of landslides, earthquakes, tidal waves and hurricanes?

The panorama of the universe is not going to heal Job but it is going to take him a long way to being healed. When he finally realises the truth he says, "I had heard of you by the hearing of the ear, but now my eye sees you."[2] God does not give a slick answer to the problem of evil, an easy soundbite which we can produce the next time someone asks us 'how can evil happen in a world created and governed by a good God?' What God does is give a revelation of himself. God brings Job to the place where the real enemy can be unmasked. Given that God is in control of the entire universe why is it filled with such suffering? Job is to see God but he is also to see the enemy and that is the beginning of healing and the beginning of the answer.

2   Job 42:5.

10

The Enemy Unmasked

Job 40-41

In the preface to one of his plays, George Bernard Shaw speaks of Job 40-41 and says, "*God really has to do better in explaining the problem of evil than to say, 'You can't make a hippopotamus, can you?*'" And that neatly encapsulates the problem of this second divine speech. If, as many commentators argue, Behemoth is the hippopotamus and Leviathan is the crocodile then we really have to ask what the fuss is about. Is God letting us down at the eleventh hour? Is there no further revelation in the book, no unmasking of the enemy? And why does Job react the way he does in 42:5? What has he seen?

It is, of course, possible to argue that the intention of the book is to leave us in mystery and to teach us that we must trust God even in the deepest darkness. That is not an unworthy idea and as we shall see, much mystery remains whatever view we take of the chapters. There are, however, a number of considerations which strongly suggest that this is not the main thrust of these two chapters.

The first is that God has already taught Job much in chapters 38-39 which we have already explored. If the Behemoth passage followed on without a break from the end of chapter 39 it would be easy to assume that it and the longer Leviathan passage were simply more of the same and were essentially reinforcing the same ideas. However, what follows in 40:1-14 is a further personal address of God to Job which implies that what follows is to be further revelation. Job has been filled with awe as God has conducted him through the cosmos. Yet he still does not know and we do not know what the place and power of evil is. There has been no kind of answer to why he is suffering. There has not yet been enlightenment about the relationship of God and evil, between God and the sinister figure who is attacking Job.

Who Is Behemoth?

Most of this chapter will be devoted to a study of Leviathan but a word is needed on Behemoth (Job 40:15-24). Behemoth is a plural form of the common Hebrew word for 'beast', often used of cattle. Since it is plain that a single figure is intended, it is probably an intensive plural i.e. The Beast par excellence. Some may recall William Golding's novel, *Lord of the Flies*, where a group of well brought up public schoolboys are marooned on a desert island where they degenerate into appalling savages and end up destroying each other. At the centre of the novel is the sinister figure of the Beast, which is both the evil inside the boys and also comes to be identified with a pig's head on a stick in a forest glade.

Here Behemoth is an embodiment of evil and chaos. I suggest that he is the personification of Death itself; death which has haunted the book and dominated Job's thoughts. In 40:13 God challenges Job about the world of death, "hide them all in the dust together, bind their faces in the world below." This prepares us for the appearance of Death itself. This is not to say that Behemoth does not have any features borrowed from the hippopotamus; this in fact serves to give him a solid reality. There are many references to myths of surrounding nations which, I have argued already, are used by the poet to illustrate profound truths about God and the world. In Egyptian legend, Seti, god of darkness, takes the form of a hippopotamus in a battle with Horus, god of light. In Canaanite myth, Mot, god of death, lurks in marshlands similar to those of 40:22-24. There is an interesting passage in Hebrews 2:14-15 where the writer says that Christ took humanity "that through death he might destroy the one who has the power of death, that is the devil, and deliver all those who through fear of death were subject to lifelong slavery." This, I suggest is what these chapters are about: Behemoth is Death and Leviathan is the one who has the power of Death, the Satan of chapters 1-2.

Job has been trying to understand this with totally inadequate criteria, the fishhook which cannot draw out Leviathan. But at least he had glimpses of the truth which is more than the Friends have done. There is no place in the Friends' universe for Behemoth and Leviathan and that is no small part of their inadequate understanding of God. As we try to grapple with this amazing description of Leviathan three questions demand attention. First of all, we must ask, who is Leviathan? It has already been suggested that he is the Satan figure but this must now be addressed in more detail. Secondly, in what sense is Leviathan part of creation and under the control of God? Thirdly, how does all this help Job and lead to the events of chapter 42?

Who Is Leviathan?

If we are serious about understanding this or indeed any other biblical text our starting point must be how would it have been understood by those who first heard or read it. There is no consensus on when the book of Job was written, but the next best thing is to study the earliest interpretations which are much more likely to be in touch with the thinking of the original audience.

When the Jewish rabbis interpreted the book they were in no doubt that these creatures were the embodiment of the powers of evil, and they built up a whole elaborate mythology of their activities from creation until the final judgment. The Greek Old Testament, the Septuagint, actually uses the word 'dragon' in place of Leviathan with obvious supernatural connotations. Indeed, nowhere, as far as I have been able to discover, do we find Behemoth and Leviathan regarded as natural creatures until the Renaissance.

In the discussion of chapters 1-2, I pointed out that one of the main problems in the interpretation of Job is where Satan goes after chapter 2. He apparently does not appear again and seems to take no further part in the action. The burden of my argument has been that he simply changes his guise. He no longer appears as the Satan but immediately he appears in 3:8 as Leviathan. And now, at the end of the poetic dialogue, we have this elaborate picture of him where so much of what has been hinted at throughout the book is about to be revealed. The Satan, master of disguise and subterfuge, disappears in his own person but re-emerges as this titanic figure of evil.

It is instructive first to examine the structure of the chapter. In 41:1-8 we have a series of rhetorical questions like those God has asked in chapters 38-39. As in these earlier chapters, the questions are designed to show the limitations of our knowledge. There is also irony and humour, "Will you play with him as with a bird, or will you put him on a leash for your girls?" (Job 41:5)

This section concludes with a statement which, like so many in Job, has both a surface meaning and hidden layers of suggestiveness, "Lay your hands on him; remember the battle— you will not do it again." (Job 41:8). Many commentators see this as an evocation of a crocodile hunt and, as I said in the comments on Behemoth, it is likely that natural creatures, in this case the crocodile, have been drawn on for some of the details. How else could we speak of supernatural creatures? Yet there is probably here a reference to the great battle with the powers of evil in some way associated with creation.

41:9-11 constitute a challenge. Leviathan is so fierce and overwhelming that even the mere sight of him will cause dread and dismay. How much greater then must be the power of God. These particular verses are very difficult to translate and are among the most obscure in the book.

The passage continues in 41:12-30 with a detailed description of Leviathan. The first thing to notice is the creature's armour. This emphasis is deliberate. In earlier chapters Job had accused God of attacking him like an armed warrior,

"He breaks me with breach upon breach; he runs upon me like a warrior." (Job 16:14)

"His troops come on together; they have cast up their siege ramp against me and encamp around my tent." (Job 19:12)

God is now unmasking the real enemy who has attacked Job like a warrior and brought his troops against him. The Lord is, in the most effective way imaginable, helping Job to see who his titanic adversary is. The supernatural aspect of Leviathan is underlined in 41:18-30, "His eyes are like the eyelids of the dawn. Out of his mouth go flaming torches; sparks of fire leap forth." The creature here becomes very much like the dragon of mediaeval legend and we are far away from the world of the crocodile.

There is also a deeper significance here which not all commentators have grasped. We have noticed already that many passages in the book such as chapters 9, 26 and 38 can be described as 'theophany' passages where the awesome power of God, always present in creation, is unveiled in earthquakes, eclipses and other massive forces of nature. Leviathan here is exposed as imitating the awesome presence of God which is so often symbolized by fire. God is saying to Job, 'Leviathan has masqueraded so subtly as me, that you have actually mistaken him for me.' It is difficult to see, even in the language of hyperbole how this can be applied to a crocodile or a whale.

The concluding verses (Job 41:31-34) speak of the creature's haunts. His sphere is the primaeval ocean, the *tehom*, the haunt of the powers of chaos and darkness. 'The sons of pride' are his acolytes and share his arrogance.

A word now about other occurrences of Leviathan in the Old Testament would be useful. Psalm 74:12ff. speaks of the power of God in creation, the power by which he separated light and darkness, sea and dry land. This is paralleled by, "You broke the heads of the sea monsters on the waters. You crushed the heads of Leviathan." The making of heaven and earth and the curbing of the forces of darkness are clearly linked. Psalm 104:26 speaking of the sea says, "There go the ships, and Leviathan which you formed to play in it." This psalm, echoing Genesis 1, speaks of the unapproachable transcendence of God in face of which Leviathan is cut down to size. Many other Psalms, such as 89 and 93, speak of God's power over the raging waters.

An interesting reference to Leviathan occurs in Isaiah 27:1, "In that day, the LORD with his hard and great and strong sword will punish Leviathan the fleeing serpent, Leviathan the twisting serpent, and he will slay the dragon that is in the sea." "That day" is the last day when evil will finally be crushed. This aspect is, of course, especially the concern of the book of Revelation where so many of the themes and images of the Old Testament are taken up and woven together. The identity of the enemy is exposed in Revelation 12:9, "And the great dragon was thrown down, that ancient serpent, who is called the devil and Satan, the deceiver of the whole world."

All this reinforces the view that Leviathan is the Satan of chapters 1-2, the ancient prince of hell, the dragon, the chaos monster also called Rahab in chapters 9 and 26 and in some other places in the Old Testament.

Satan Under the Control of God

In what sense is Leviathan part of nature and under the control of God? A good starting point is Isaiah 45:7, "I form light and create darkness; I make well-being and create calamity; I am the LORD who does all these things." This is a useful reminder that in chapters 1-2 God not only allows but actually incites and encourages Satan to proceed against Job.

But in what sense is God in control, and what does it mean to say that he created Behemoth and Leviathan? They are God's creatures; the powers of evil are part of creation. In Genesis 1 God creates heaven and earth which are described as 'good'. What place is there for the 'formlessness' and 'void' also mentioned?

Now this is not simply an Old Testament problem. John 1:3 states "All things were made through him, and without him was not anything made that was made." And this, of course, means that death, sickness, evil and chaos must in some mysterious way be under God's control and part of his creation.

The only viable alternative is dualism. Dualism essentially argues that the powers of light and darkness are equal and co-exist for ever. This seems plausible when we observe the world around us or look at history. The swing of the pendulum between good and evil in life at all levels seems unending.

But that view is in every single respect unbiblical and leaves no gospel. It is unbiblical about creation, because there is in fact no creation, simply an unending struggle between the forces of good and evil. There is no event in the middle of history which deals the deathblow to Satan and sin. There is no final salvation because good and evil are doomed to fight for ever in sickening, see-saw equilibrium.

But there is another way to look at the evidence. The Bible unequivocally states that God created everything including the Satan. Consider what God does in the act of creation: he breathes life into creatures other than himself, and by breathing his life into them, he gives them the capacity for choice, which includes the capacity to disobey him. Thus the Satan and the powers of darkness were created by God but not as evil creatures.

The Old Testament hints at this in picture and imagery rather than by direct statement. It speaks of a spirit, created glorious and magnificent, but who, puffed up with pride, wished to be God — the ultimate sin of a creature.

In Isaiah 14 we read of a mysterious figure who on one level is the literal king of Babylon who is "brought down to Sheol, to the far reaches of the pit" (Isaiah 14:15). But the language used of this figure who wishes to "ascend above the heights of the clouds", and "make himself like the Most High" goes far beyond any earthly potentate. It suggests a far more sinister power behind earthly powers using his great intelligence to frustrate God's purposes.

Likewise in Ezekiel 26 and 28 we read of the Prince of Tyre, and this is part of Ezekiel's oracles against the various nations prominent at the time. Yet once again the language goes far beyond that of any Tyrian leader,

> *"You were the signet of perfection,*
> *Full of wisdom and perfect in beauty.*
> *You were in Eden, the garden of God.*
> *You were an anointed guardian cherub.*
> *I placed you, you were on the holy mountain of God.*
> *In the midst of the stones of fire you walked.*

You were blameless in all your ways
From the day you were created,
Till unrighteousness was found in you."
(Ezekiel 28:12; 13a, 14-15)

It seems to me that what we have here is a depiction of a spirit of great power, great beauty and great intelligence who falls and uses these attributes against God and his purposes. Milton, in *Paradise Lost*, develops with great insight and imagination the magnificence of this figure. And that has been the thrust of my argument about Job 41, that God's enemy is still a magnificent figure and is all the more dangerous for that.

But there is another aspect to all this. Genesis 3 speaks of another fall— the fall of human beings. Eve was tempted by the serpent, but who is the serpent? In one sense he is a snake, a creature, but no Hebrew reader would fail to recognize the nuances of the word. The Hebrew word *nahash*, which is used there of the serpent, is used in Job 26:13, and in the Psalter, of Leviathan. That is the evil power which is active in Genesis 3. And it is not only humankind which is corrupted but the earth is spoiled as well and will produce thorns and thistles.

This is a theme Paul elaborates in Romans 8 when he speaks of the redemption of the whole universe, "For we know that the whole creation has been groaning together in the pains of childbirth until now." (Romans 8:22). Creation groans and waits for its renewal which will follow the glorifying of the children of God. Evil now haunts the created order but will not do so forever.

In chapters 38-39 God had said to Job, 'You must look at the creation the way that I look at it. You must realise that the universe in all its heights and depths is under my control. And in chapters 40-41 the powers of evil are under my control as well and will ultimately serve my good purposes.' Even Leviathan will ultimately serve providence; the devil, as Luther said, is God's devil.

How Does This Help Job?

In chapter 42:5 Job finds this revelation astonishing and describes it as the contrast between seeing God and hearing about him, "I had heard of you by the hearing of the ear, but now my eye sees you." Two things in particular are worth noting.

First of all, Job has seen the awesome power of evil. Never again would he be unaware of the nature of the powers of darkness. We have already noticed that he had glimpsed something of this reality, notably in 9:24, "If it is not he, then who is it?" We have also noticed that it was ignorance of this dimension which was one of the factors which caused the Friends to misunderstand Job's situation so badly.

But the second and more important thing is that Job has seen that God is in control of the powers of evil. God knows this creature so intimately and describes him in such detail that he cannot fail to be in control. Much mystery remains and Job does not see everything. Yet he now knows that God is in complete control. As Christians we need to know that the most important thing about the devil is that Jesus Christ has defeated him.

A man walking through Berlin in the months immediately following the end of the Second World War passed the ruins of Hitler's Chancellery, the very place where monstrous evil had been hatched. It was a beautiful day, the sun was shining and a young mother was sitting on the steps of the chancellery feeding her child. Just as the man was passing the child threw his head back and laughed and his shadow fell across the ruins of that sinister building. So it is that the shadow of another child falls across the grim empire of darkness. So it is that by taking our flesh and by the cross and the resurrection Christ has broken the vicious spiral of evil and made victory possible for his followers.[1]

---

1 The argument of chapter 10 is developed in detail in my book, 'Now my eyes have seen you: images of creation and evil in the book of Job'. IVP. NSBT. 2002 esp. pp. 117-174 which include my own translation of the Behemoth and Leviathan passages.

11

The Vision Glorious

Job 42

Many people have felt a sense of anti-climax on coming to Job 42. After the titanic struggles, the volcanic energy and the brilliant imagery of the previous chapters we seem to have entered a rather smug world of an improving tale with a conventional happy ending. Worse still is the lurking feeling that the old 'prosperity theology' has been let in the back door. Some have solved this problem by simply arguing that the chapter, especially 42:7-17 have been added by a pious but naïve and ungifted writer, rather like some 18th century critics who rewrote Shakespeare's *King Lear* to give it a happy ending.

But, as so often in the book of Job, when we make hasty responses we find that the rug is pulled from under our feet and we are left gasping at the brilliance and profundity of the author, and wiser and more humble if we will listen. Far from being an anti-climax, this chapter is a necessary concluding movement and has numerous links with what has gone before. We shall look first at Job's response to the Lord, with particular emphasis on what he means by 'seeing' God. Then we shall examine in what sense Job has 'spoken right' about God and the Friends have not. Finally we shall explore the 'happy ending' and consider whether it is a satisfactory conclusion to the book.

We have already seen how God's second speech with its unveiling of supernatural evil embodied in Behemoth and Leviathan is the climax of the theology of the book. Job's response here in 42:1-6 is particularly related to that. Leviathan and his place in God's universe has been a demonstration to Job that no part of creation and no creature, however powerful, was outside the Lord's domain. The great mysteries, the farthest reaches of space and time, the thunder and lightning, the predatory beasts, the underworld itself remain full of unsolved problems, but God has demonstrated he is in control. Job could now look up at the night sky and into the depths of the ocean knowing that the God who made it all is good and had good purposes for him.

Job's Response of Humility and Faith

The effect of all this on Job is demonstrated in two ways. First in 42:3-4 he confesses his limitations and acknowledges the truth of God's words. It is important to notice that he does not confess sins that he did not commit, his integrity remains and God himself does not challenge this. What he does admit is ignorance and presumption. He realises that his knowledge and insight have been limited and partial and by quoting God's own words, "Who is this that hides counsel without knowledge?" he shows that he has fully accepted the revelation he has been given in chapters 38-41.

But Job goes beyond confession and in 42:5-6 he expresses positively his newborn faith and confidence. In particular he draws a contrast between hearing and seeing. Hearing was not to be despised; it was a necessary part of the journey, but the final goal was not to be the hearing of new insights but the vision of God himself. What does Job 'see'? This must be related to 19:26-27, "In my flesh I shall see God, whom I shall see for myself, and my eyes shall behold and not another." We noticed in our discussion of that passage that seeing God was more important than establishing the specific time when this would happen. God, by appearing now, has vindicated Job's integrity and demonstrated that his purposes for Job are good and loving. Job has 'seen' the universe, including the underworld, with God as his guide and that has been a revelation not just of creation but of the Creator.

In the creation story in Genesis 1, a major factor in the creative process is that God 'saw.' There 'seeing' is not a casual glance but an affirming that God continually looks on, cares for and provides for his creation. One day Job will see as God sees.

Another significant point is that this vision of God, like the vision that Isaiah saw in the temple (Isaiah 6), makes him realise his unworthiness. This leads to action, symbolised by dust and ashes. We should not misunderstand the word 'repent' (Job 42:6). This does not mean that Job was guilty after all and is now acknowledging, in effect, that the Friends were right and that he needed to confess all kinds of secret sins. A more helpful comparison is with Abraham in Genesis 18:27, "Now that I have been so bold as to speak to the LORD, though I am nothing but dust and ashes." There Abraham is interceding for Sodom, as Job is about to intercede for the Friends. Job repents, not because he has been wicked but because he has been presumptuous.[1] Yet, like Abraham, he is a righteous man and nowhere is the righteous man more effective than on his knees.

Moreover, at the beginning of the book, Job's isolation from society has been symbolised by sitting among the ashes (Job 2:8). Now the same symbol is used for a restored relationship with God which opens the way for a restored relationship with others. It is to this restoration we now turn.

Job's Vindication and Restoration

The Epilogue (Job 42:7-17) corresponds to the Prologue (Job 1-2) and reverts to narrative which completes the story. The most striking feature of 42:7-9 is God's condemnation of the Friends, "you have not spoken of me what is right, as my servant Job has." But has not Job said some dreadful things about God which we have already noted on our journey through the book? We may recall some of Job's bitter words, such as:

"God gives me up to the ungodly... I was at ease, and he broke me apart; he seized me by the neck and dashed me to pieces." (Job 16:11-12)

"He breaks me down on every side, and I am gone, and my hope he has pulled up like a tree." (Job 19:10)

The Friends, on the other hand, have spoken the language of pious orthodoxy. Yet, as we have noticed, they imagine that they can put God's case better than he can himself. They have shown an unfeeling arrogance and a stupefying complacency.

---

1   See Ralph Davis' helpful and penetrating comments in his *The Word Became Fresh*, Christian Focus, Mentor, 2006. pp.111-114.

In what sense has Job 'spoken what is right' about God? In the first place he has realised that what matters is not simply knowing and saying the right things, but having a relationship with God. In all of his anger and confusion he has held on to this determination to see and know God. This is an encouragement to all who find God's ways puzzling and perplexing, especially if they are being chided for their lack of faith. God is far kinder than many of his followers and far more ready to welcome an honest searcher than some of his self-appointed spokesmen are.

Also, Job has shown glimpses from time to time of the supernatural origin and nature of his sufferings, "If it is not he, then who is it?" (Job 9:24). It is these insights which God has built on and put into their true perspective in chapters 38-41.

Thus the relationship is restored with God and reconciliation with the Friends follows. Job's sacrifice and prayer is used by God in the restoration. It is also significant that God three times here calls Job "my servant." We saw earlier how this is not simply a regular term for the faithful but is particularly applied to figures like Moses and David and suggests a specially close relationship of love and obedience. Nothing could show more clearly that Job has come through into the sunshine. Not that he had ever ceased to be God's servant, but this is now being publicly acknowledged as God had initially acknowledged it to the Satan himself.

God has publicly vindicated Job, he has shown that all the cruel and insensitive attacks on his integrity by the Friends have been false. He has shown that he does reward anguished protest and honest seeking. Just as the mysterious depths of the universe, the habits of mountain goats and even the fearsome Behemoth and Leviathan are in his hands, so the labyrinthine depths of human experience are known to him and can be handled by him.

But what are we to make of the 'happy ending' in 42:7-17? Inevitably there is a lowering of tension and an absence of the volcanic energy of the rest of the book. After all it is tense situations, cliff-hangers and the like which give excitement and suspense to a story. The writer is now showing the vindication of Job's faith in the everyday world.

Some things need to be said to put this into context. The first is that Job wins through to a restored relationship with God and with others before God restores his fortunes. There is no question of a bargain here in which Job repents because Yahweh has blessed him. Nor is God blessing Job as a reward for his words of contrition. Rather, Job realises that it is God himself who is the real reward. With robust faith Job had said "The LORD gave, and the LORD has taken away; blessed be the name of the LORD." (Job 1:21). Now he is returning to that faith in God himself which is ultimately not dependent on his giving or withholding.

What is happening here is very like a pattern we can find in many of the Lament Psalms where the psalmist pours out his agony to God and then, without any apparent change in circumstances, triumphantly affirms God's goodness. A good example of this is Psalm 22 which begins with the words, "My God, my God why have you forsaken me?" but there is a triumphant affirmation of faith, "I will declare your name to my brothers; in the congregation I will praise you." (Psalm 22:22). So here, Job, without knowing that his fortunes will be restored, renews his faith and confidence in God.

The phrase "the LORD restored the fortunes of Job" (Job 42:10) is significant. Elsewhere it refers to the restoration of the nation, especially to the return of Israel from exile. "Days are coming, declares the LORD, when I will restore the fortunes of my people, Israel and Judah, says the LORD, and I will bring them back to the land that I gave to their fathers" (Jeremiah 30:3). Throughout the Psalms God is continually praised as the Creator and Saviour, and the saving act particularly celebrated is the Exodus. Over and over these great realities cause rejoicing, "My help comes from the LORD, the maker of heaven and earth" (Psalm 121:2). "When the LORD brought back the captives to Zion, we were like men who dream" (Psalm 126:1). Something of the sort is happening here; Job has seen the great panorama of God's power and now applies that to his own situation.

This return to normality is symbolized by a shared meal (Job 42:11). This is the first note of celebration since chapter 1. Then Yahweh "blessed the latter days of Job more than his beginning" (Job 42:12). His family and possessions are restored abundantly and his life stretches out to the kind of length associated with the days of the patriarchs.

What is important to notice here is that the security Job now enjoys is in God himself. There is no more security in the new family and possessions than the old one. In other words there is still need for faith and the vision of God. The point is that the faith Job now has is incalculably deeper than it was in chapter 1. Job's life still has many years to run, one hundred and forty, in fact, and no guarantee is given that these years will be trouble free.

Three things can be said to sum up this chapter.

The first is that earthly blessing and prosperity are important, particularly in the Old Testament world where the full light of the Resurrection was not yet known. The blessing God gives here: family, wealth and renewed prosperity are good in themselves and, while not rewards for good conduct, are gifts of grace. These are the very blessings for which we regularly pray and which form a large part of our lives.

Secondly, this chapter emphasizes the importance of right relationships. Ultimately what matters is knowing God and that leads to the healing of relationships with others. Suffering has refined Job and released hidden depths in him, yet his intercession for the Friends is of a piece with his intercession for his family at the beginning. Job had earlier said, "But he knows the way that I take; when he has tried me, I shall come out as gold" (Job 23:10). All the way Job has longed for and fought for a new understanding and closer relationship with God and this is what he has now been given.

And the third thing is the emphasis on God's creating power and his renewing love. All through the book the question of God the Creator and his purposes has been at the very heart of the debate. Job has never doubted the awesome power of God, what he has often doubted was that his purposes were loving. Chapter 42 illustrates and emphasises God's love in the most striking way. The emphasis on 'restoring fortunes' and 'blessing' is one of the most notable features of the chapter and these words are full of the sense of God's creating and sustaining power. The number of livestock reinforce the sense of vibrant and abundant life reminiscent of the creation story in Genesis 1. Similarly, the beauty of Job's daughters, remind us of how God looked on creation and pronounced it good.

So the book ends with the death of Job at a ripe old age surrounded by his family. In the next chapter we shall look at the light thrown on the book of Job by the New Testament.

12

Job Revisited

Many years ago, Dr. G. Campbell Morgan,[1] wrote a book called *The Answers of Jesus to Job*. He took many of the cries of Job and showed that the only answer to these is to be found in Jesus himself.

The purpose of this present book has been rather different; it has been to take the book of Job on its own terms, and while frequent reference has been made to the New Testament, my main concern has been to expound the message of Job as it stands. However, it would be helpful to say something of the place of the book, not just in the Old Testament but in the canon of Scripture as a whole.

A Christian reading of Job sees it in the light of the Cross and the Empty Tomb. It is also important to see it in the light of Jesus' teaching about the Kingdom of God and the radical and uncomfortable question mark this places against many of our assumptions.

To make this a manageable topic I thought it would be useful to concentrate on the Gospel of Mark. I choose this for two reasons.

1   He was a noted preacher and author in the late 19th and early 20th century and was minister of Westminster Chapel, London, for two periods in the first part of the 20th century.

First, in Mark the gospel is expressed in its briefest and most concentrated form and the issues raised most starkly. Second, a particular emphasis of Mark is on Jesus as the Suffering Servant. Few Old Testament passages are closer to Job than Isaiah 53 with its moving and profound picture of the Servant who is the Sufferer.

What I want to do is to look at some of the main aspects of Mark's teaching about Jesus and say something of how they throw light on the questions the Job poet grapples with. This will help us to reflect further on the problems raised by the Old Testament book.

Five issues will be explored: Jesus' preaching of the Kingdom; the activities of Satan; Jesus' miracles; his death and his resurrection.

Jesus' Preaching of the Kingdom

The term 'Kingdom of God', while rooted in the Old Testament, is not used in Job itself; yet the issues raised by it are at the heart of what Job is about. The life Job lives in chapter 1 (more fully described in chapter 29) is an example of the kind of lifestyle of someone who is expressing the rule of God in his life. It is a life marked by righteousness and justice and enjoys the smile of God's blessing. But there are deeper connotations as well. The kingdom comes by suffering and apparent disaster; it has already come in Jesus but not fully revealed until he returns in glory.

Moreover. Jesus in Mark, like Job is popular and admired at the beginning. This is seen in such statements as "everyone is looking for you" (Mark 1:37); "people were coming to him from every quarter" (Mark 1:45); "A very large crowd gathered around him, so that he got into a boat" (Mark 4:1). However, a startling reversal has taken place by the Passion narratives where Mark particularly emphasises the utter loneliness and isolation of Jesus (Mark 14-15).

It is not difficult to see parallels to this in the experience of Job as a glance at chapters 29-30 will demonstrate. Chapter 29 gives a glowing picture of Job's earlier life, "When God watched over me, when his lamp shone upon my head" (Job 29:2-3). Indeed this whole chapter is an illustration of God's kingdom in action. Job rescues the poor and fatherless (Job 29:12); he cares for the disabled (Job 29:15) and he speaks with authority, "Men listened to me and waited and kept silence for my counsel" (Job 29:21), just as Jesus spoke with authority (Mark 1:27). Yet by chapter 30 terror and isolation have replaced peace and community, "Terrors are turned upon me; my honour is pursued as by the wind, and my prosperity has passed away like a cloud" (Job 30:15).

Two observations follow from this. The first is that living the life of God's kingdom in this world will often involve suffering and isolation. The Friends of Job did not grasp this and advocated a simplistic link between goodness and prosperity. The growing hostility to Jesus shows that far from disaster being a sign of God's displeasure it is rather an inevitable part of the coming of the kingdom, "For whoever would save his life will lose it, but whoever loses his life for my sake and the gospel's will save it" (Mark 8:35). Job, in fact, in his innocent suffering and misrepresentation to which he is subjected is a very clear picture of Christ himself.

The other observation is that the suffering must be seen in the wider perspective of the purposes of God. In Mark 14:62, "Jesus said... you will see the Son of Man seated at the right hand of Power and coming with the clouds of heaven." Thus the hardship is placed in a much wider context as God puts Job's suffering in such a context in chapters 38-42. So we find that both Testaments speak with one voice on how suffering and glory belong together.

The Activity of Satan

But Mark, like Job, sees far deeper causes behind suffering than simple misfortune. We come to the second area of consideration which is the role of Satan who appears early in Mark as he does in Job. Moreover, once again Satan's initiative is intertwined with that of God, "The Spirit immediately drove him out into the wilderness. And he was in the wilderness forty days, being tempted by Satan" (Mark 1:12-13).

The New Testament elsewhere draws an important connection between the coming of the kingdom and the defeat of Satan, "The reason the Son of God appeared was to destroy the works of the devil" (1 John 3:8). This both underlines the reality of the demonic and the necessity of God's own intervention in dealing with it. This intervention of Satan at the beginning of Jesus' ministry is an attempt to deflect God's servant (a word used of Job as well as Jesus) from his appointed path.

As in Job, the assaults of Satan continue in a virulent way. There is the interesting passage in Mark 3:22-30 where the scribes come from Jerusalem and say that Jesus is "possessed by Beelzebul, and by the prince of demons he casts out the demons."

This is a fascinating parallel with some passages in Job where the Friends accuse him of belonging to that sinister underworld (notice especially Bildad's speech about the 'king of terrors' in chapter 18).

But most striking is the reference in the Gethsemane narrative, "And he took with him Peter and James and John, and began to be greatly distressed and troubled. And he said to them, 'My soul is very sorrowful, even to death'" (Mark 14:33-34). The words translated 'greatly distressed and 'troubled' are very strong indeed and suggest a kind of shrinking horror and dismay. Moreover, there is the suggestion of powerful, unseen, supernatural presences, of death and Satan pressing in on Jesus as the devil returns to avenge the defeats suffered in the wilderness and Galilee and numerous other places.

What these passages indicate is that attack by Satan is inescapable in the endeavour to serve God. The inadequacy of Job's Friends' explanations of his calamities is even more starkly underlined. Jesus himself met such conflict and was subjected to similar misrepresentation. It is necessary, therefore, to realise and account for the presence of the demonic. Failure to do this led Job's Friends to regard him as suffering punishment for evil and Job himself to misunderstand God's purposes.

The Miracles of Jesus

The whole theme of the supernatural is present in the Marcan account of Jesus' miracles. To make this third area manageable I shall concentrate on two miracles: Jesus stilling the storm (Mark 4:35-41) and the healing of a demon-possessed man (Mark 5:1-20).

In Job, as we have seen, the untamed sea is a symbol of the powers of chaos and evil which only God can control. In Mark (and in the corresponding passages in Matthew 8:23-27 and Luke 8:22-25) Jesus' rebuke of the sea is followed by the casting out of the demons from the tormented man and the precipitate descent of the pigs into the sea. These two stories plainly belong together and underline the connection made in Job and elsewhere in the Old Testament between the evil spirits and the sea.

One or two points are worth noting. The first is that the verb Jesus uses to rebuke the sea in Mark 4:39 (*epitemesen*) is used of rebuking an evil spirit in Mark 1:25. Thus it is plain that Jesus is commanding an evil power to be silent. This is confirmed by the other verb in Mark 4:39 (*pephimoso*) 'be still' (also used in Mark 1:25). Jesus here is challenging the power of darkness by the power of the Kingdom.

This explains the awestruck question of the disciples in 4:21, "Who then is this that even the wind and the sea obey him?" Now this story comes in a series of mighty acts: exorcism, healing, unprecedented authority in preaching. All of these, of course, have many Old Testament parallels: Saul's evil spirit banished by David's playing; healings and even raising the dead by Elijah and Elisha; the inspired utterances of the prophets. Thus there was inevitable controversy (most of it reflected within the disciples themselves) about who Jesus of Nazareth was. Most of his mighty acts were not unique, but surely there was only one who could say to the raging sea, "Thus far shall you come, and no farther, and here shall your proud waves be stayed" (Job 38:11).

Central to the miracles of Jesus is his authority over the whole of creation and the 'principalities and powers.' We have already seen how Job's life became the battleground of spiritual powers and that we are dealing not merely with misfortune but with the deepest issues of creation, evil, life and death. Only in Jesus who not only suffers terrible agony like Job, but also brings life out of them, can we truly find answers to the huge problems raised by the Old Testament book.

The Death of Jesus

And that brings us to our fourth area which is the passion and death of our Lord. In Mark the isolation and anguish of Jesus are powerfully conveyed. In the Gethsemane narrative, already mentioned, Mark underlines Jesus' complete loneliness. In Luke's account of the event, "And there appeared to him an angel from heaven, strengthening him." (Luke 22:43). Also in Luke 23:26-31, women follow and sympathise with Jesus, in Mark 15:40 they 'were watching from a distance.' But far worse is the cry of dereliction, "My God, my God, why have you forsaken me?" (Mark 15:34).

When we compare this with the experience of Job we find many parallels. Particularly poignant is Job 19:13-14, "He has put my brothers far from me, and those who know me are wholly estranged from me. My relatives have failed me, my close Friends have forgotten me".

In that passage the terrible isolation that Job feels is intensified by the thought that it is God himself who has brought this isolation on him. Similarly Job speaks of the hatred and contempt of those who once respected him, "They abhor me; they keep aloof from me; they do not hesitate to spit at the sight of me." (Job 30:10). To isolation has been added ridicule and mockery, similar grim details as we have in Mark 15:16-20.

These comparisons are obvious enough and illustrate again the way in which Jesus totally identified himself with suffering humanity. If that were all, however, the depiction of suffering both in Job and Mark would remain a powerful statement of human agony and distress but would not point to any answers.

Two important details, however, in Mark's account throw light on the situation in Job. The first is the tearing of the curtain of the temple from top to bottom (Mark 15:38) symbolising that there is now free access to the presence of God. Because Jesus' suffering gathers into it all the sin and suffering of the ages, others can now approach God through his sacrifice. Job's longing for a mediator and for access to the heavenly court now finds its answer.

The other is the words of the centurion, 'Truly this man was the Son of God.' (Mark 15:39). This is a moment of revelation, comparable to "I had heard of you by the hearing of the ear, but now my eye sees you." (Job 42:5). In both cases insight and vision follow tragedy and suffering.

The Resurrection of Jesus

One more topic remains. We have already noted, especially in the discussion of Job 19, how Job had glimpses of something, or rather someone, beyond death itself who would put everything right in the heavenly court. Not until the Resurrection of Jesus, however, could that hope be clearly focused and realised. We have looked, in the context of the book itself, at Job's great leap of faith in 19:25, "I know that my Redeemer lives, and at the last he will stand upon the earth."

Without the Resurrection these words remain ultimately a pious wish. Only the words of Mark 16:6 give them content, "He has risen; he is not here. See the place where they laid him." It is this event which makes sense of all the unsatisfied longings and cries of agony from Job and others.

There is one specific aspect of Mark's Resurrection account which is particularly relevant to Job. Most scholars agree that Mark originally ended his Gospel at 16:8, "And they went out and fled from the tomb, for trembling and astonishment had seized them, and they said nothing to anyone, for they were afraid."

This very vividly reminds us that this event was beyond human understanding and thus caused fear and trembling. Mark has frequently underlined the confusion and fear that people felt as they had not been able to understand who Jesus is. To put it another way: the fact that Christ is risen still requires the response of faith and humility. Similarly, we noticed that at the end of the book, Job still needs to trust God. The life, death and resurrection of Jesus both echoes Job's sufferings and points to their solution.

One or two observations will be helpful in summing up. It is plain that suffering is an integral part of what it means to be God's servant. God describes Job as 'my servant' and Jesus is presented as Isaiah's 'Suffering Servant'. In both cases Satan attacks and the whole basis of their dependence on God is questioned. To be a servant is to run the risk of encountering a hostile and dangerous world where all the familiar certainties will dissolve. This does not mean that the servant has been unfaithful; in some mysterious way faithfulness is tested and strengthened by adversity, "But he knows the way that I take; when he has tried me I shall come out as gold." (Job 23:10).

A related theme is that Jesus is not only another servant of God, but the Servant who is God himself and whose self-giving not only exemplifies but heals the suffering of other servants. We looked earlier at Job's cries for an advocate in the heavenly court culminating in chapter 19. In Jesus, that advocate who is also the suffering servant is found.

George Herbert in his poem *The Collar* chafes like Job under God's discipline, but through the suffering eventually hears and welcomes a well-loved voice,

> *I struck the board, and cried,' No more'*
> *I will abroad....*
> *But as I raved and grew more fierce and wild*
> *At every word,*
> *Me thought I heard one calling, 'Child.'*
> *And I replied 'My Lord.'*

13

Preaching on Job

I have added this chapter and hope it will be helpful to those who preach and teach Job. Many find this daunting for a number of reasons. First is its length but no more so than some of the prophetic and historical books. It would probably be a mistake to preach forty two sermons. Sometimes large chunks could be treated together and always keep in mind the flow and structure of the book.

A related problem is what to do with the extensive speeches of the Friends since so much of what they say is wrongheaded. I have tried earlier to show how we can learn what to avoid which is an important part of coming to the truth.

A third issue is that we need to remember the underlying emphasis of the book on the mystery of evil and suffering in a universe created and sustained by a loving God. It, of course, is concerned with the problem of innocent suffering but that must not be isolated from these bigger issues.

What I shall do in this chapter is to suggest a series for Sunday preaching and then a shorter series for a conference. Thinking of a title for a series is important; not that we can sum up a book in a soundbite but that a title can focus thoughts on the direction of travel. I would suggest two possible titles. The first one is the title of this book, '*How God Treats his Friends*' and the second is '*God Moves in a Mysterious Way.*' The reason for these suggestions is that both focus on God as well as suggesting mysteries and problems.

Sunday Preaching

Since the book originally grew from talks at a Christian Union, I am largely following the order in the book but more specifically looking at how the material might be presented.

Sermon 1. Is God the Author of Evil? (Chapters 1-2)

A brief introduction on Wisdom Literature and its place in the canon – Job, like the rest of the Wisdom Literature (Proverbs, Ecclesiastes, Song of Songs) draws on Genesis 1-11. Thus the emphasis is not on Israel's history and religion but on creation, the nature of humanity, the Fall and evil and suffering and the like.

1. *Receiving good and evil*: Blessed but battered, not as result of sin but of evil and fallenness – real faith and real suffering – Job is not passive – he suffers but does not sin with his lips – he is the man of Psalm 1.
2. *Ruling justly*: God's mysterious providence – encapsulated in 2:10 – place of heavenly court or divine council – God ultimately in control.
3. *Raging relentlessly*: Satan attacks Job to get at God – evil is powerful but operates only under God's permission (1:12; 2:6).

Sermon 2. Where Is God in the Agony? (Chapter 3)

Powerful soliloquy introduces the poetry which rolls its majestic way for nearly 40 chapters – compare Psalm 86 and the Gethsemane story.

Questions to explore the chapter:

1. *What is happening to Job?* – powerful images which run throughout the book – 'Sheol'; the powers of darkness; the apparent hostility of God – Job longs for creation to disappear.
2. *Why is this happening to Job?* – the inevitable feeling of abandonment; the silence of the Friends; the attack of Satan on his thoughts and imagination and worse the apparent hostility of God.
3. *What hope is there for Job?* – we cannot jump to chapter 42 but two points can be made: God is in control although that is more terrifying than reassuring at this point; Job's utter honesty – like Jacob in Genesis 32 he will not let God go.

Sermon 3. Who Needs Enemies? (Chapters 4-11)

One way of treating the Friends' speeches is to look for themes rather than attempt to expound each chapter in turn Here we see what to avoid.

1. *They do not listen* – either to God or Job.
2. *They do not discern the activity of Satan.*
3. *Their God is too small.*

Sermon 4. "If It Is Not He, Then Who Is It?" (Chapter 9)

Powerful combination of liturgical and legal language – Job the worshipper and Job the litigant wrestle with mysteries – focus on Job's great insight at the end of 9:24.

1. *Where is God in the created order?* (9:1-13) – language echoing Psalm 46 – the evil in creation (9:8 & 13) – the mystery of the starry heavens (9:9-10).
2. *Where is God in society?* (9:14-24) – human world reflects the questions of the material world – capacity for outrage – mystery of oppression and injustice as in many of the psalms.
3. *Where is God in Job's circumstances?* (9:25-35) – first hint of an arbiter.

Sermon 5. An Advocate in Heaven. (Chapter 19)

Look at the context – the sense of increasing hostility and isolation – then concentrate on 19:23-27.

1. *Who is the Redeemer?* – explore the concept of kinsman redeemer illustrated in the book of Ruth – who but God can negotiate with God?
2. *What will the Redeemer do?* 'stand on the dust' as the Living One who has conquered death – NB repetition of 'seeing' – he will not be a stranger.

This is a rich passage and needs careful analysis and robust presentation.

Sermon 6. Not Speaking What Is Right. (Chapters 15-25)

This is a further consideration of the Friends and their later speeches where the tone becomes more heated and the condemnation of Job more bitter. It is important to emphasise that while most of what the Friends say is wrong the material matters because exposure of error is vital in establishing the truth just as the prophets and the apostles spend a lot of time denouncing false teaching.

> 1. *Belittling Job* – 'windy knowledge' (e.g. Job 15:2)
> 2. *Vindictiveness* – (e.g. Job 18 and 20)
> 3. *Narrow piety* – (e.g. Job 25)

These are some of the ways the Friends condemn Job and exemplify what we need to avoid. They are not always wrong, but they are on the main things; Job is not always right, but he is on the main things.

Sermon 7. Where Can Wisdom Be Found? (Chapter 28)

A calmer staging post as the voices of the Friends die away and is a kind of summing-up (as indeed all of Job 26-31 are) of the journey travelled with glimpses of the destination – the chapter unfolds in three movements:

> 1. *A profound search* (28:1-11) – metaphor of mining with echoes of Sheol as an echo of Job's experience – human achievements magnificent but not adequate.
> 2. *A humble acknowledgment* (28:12-22) – wisdom will not be found by ransacking the physical universe – nor can it be bought – the mystery lies beyond the realm of death (28:22)

3. *A wise God* (28:23-28) – God controls elusive mysteries and cares about wise living – 28:28 echoes 1:1 raising inevitable questions.

Sermon 8. Apologetic Which Fails to Reach the Heart. (Chapters 32-37)

Elihu is an angry young man and full of words – he says many good things but shows no empathy or sensitivity. Truth needs to be presented in love. Job does not doubt the majesty of God but sees God as hostile. There is no sense of his own sinfulness.

Sermon 9. The Grandeur of God. (Chapters 38-39)

Finally the Lord appears and he is asking the questions.

Job is presumptuous but not a secret sinner.

God is not giving easy solutions to the tragedies of chapters 1-2 but placing them in the big picture. Thus there is the sense of the vastness and value of the created order but also mysteries of darkness and cruelty.

1. *God makes and knows all he makes.*
2. *God cares and sustains.*
3. *God is to be praised.*

Sermon 10. The Enemy Unmasked. (Chapters 40-41)

Here we are shown death and him who has the power of death and the question of cosmic evil is addressed.

A sermon on Leviathan might look something like this:

1. *The formidable enemy* (41:1-11) – don't treat him lightly.
2. *The frightening appearance* (41:12-30) – parody of God himself.
3. *The fearless creature* (41:31-34) – yes, the above is true but he is not the Creator.

Sermon 11. The Vision Glorious. (Chapter 42)

Job's response of humility and faith. Job's vindication and restoration.

Yes Job dies but 'full of days' – the OT blessing points to endless days in the new creation.

Short Series Outline

The following could be for a conference or if you want to give an overview of the whole book. I suggest a possible four part series:

1. *God tests his servant to the limits*: This is the prologue (chs. 1–2) which outline the basic story. We would look at the place of the book in Wisdom Literature; the narrative techniques; the interplay of God, Job and Satan; the arrival of the Friends; the place of suffering; the apparent unfairness.

2. *God perplexes his servant*: This involves an exploration of the great issues in the poetic dialogue (chs. 32-37) and would need a careful selection of details. The weaknesses in the contributions of the Friends and Elihu would be explored as would Job's many insights. Such chapters as 9, 19 and 28 would be given special emphasis.

3. *God reveals himself to his servant*: The divine speeches in chapters 38-41 are the subject. The revelation in the created order and in the world of the supernatural would be explored. It is important to see how this relates to earlier parts of the book.

4. *God vindicates his servant*: Chapter 42 shows Job's restoration and vindication as well as concluding the narrative. Explore the ways in which these happen.

These suggestions are not, of course, the only way to tackle the book and preachers will need to work out what helps them. In any case, preach Job.

Further Reading

Of making many books on Job there is no end!
Here are a few for those who want to explore more deeply:

Andersen, Frances I. *Job: An Introduction and Commentary*. Tyndale Old Testament Commentaries, Leicester, InterVarsity Press, 1976.

Ash, Christopher. *Out of the storm: Grappling with God in the Book of Job*. InterVarsity Press, 2004.

Ash, Christopher. *Job: The Wisdom of the Cross*. Preaching the Word Commentary, Series Edited by R. Kent Hughes, Crossway, 2014.

Fyall, Robert S. *Now My Eyes Have Seen You: Images of creation and evil in the Book of Job*. New Studies in Biblical Theology, Series Edited by D. A. Carson, InterVarsity Press, 2002.

Habel, Norman C. *The Book of Job*. A Commentary, Old Testament Library, Westminster/John Knox Press,U.S., 1985.

Hartley, John E. *The Book of Job*. New International Commentary on the Old Testament, Wm. B. Eerdmans Publishing Co., Grand Rapids, Michigan, 1988.

Pope, Marvin H. *Job: A New Translation with Introduction, Translation and Commentary*. The Anchor Bible, Yale University Press, Garden City, 1965.

The
TRON
Church

Our church is part of the worldwide family united by the cross of Jesus. Students, young workers, families and older saints, from many nationalities and all walks of life – we are all one in Christ Jesus.

Our vision, which drives everything we do, is to see the risen Lord Jesus crowded by people from our city and every nation, ransomed by his blood and raised by his Spirit through the gospel, reigning for eternity with him to the glory of God the Father.

So we worship together to make and grow mature disciples of Jesus Christ in ever greater numbers who with us will glorify God and enjoy him forever.

We are a presbyterian church and are committed and accountable to a wider family of congregations in Scotland called the Didasko Presbytery.

If you are visiting Glasgow, do be sure to visit us on a Sunday.

For more information, visit our website - tron.church

TRON BOOKS

Launched in 2024, Tron Books seeks to produce and distribute excellent Christian books that both equip and encourage church leaders and members. Our hope is to publish a range of biblically-faithful, stimulating and timeless publications that will help those in the pulpit or pew to prosper in their Christian walk and service.

To find out more, visit our website - tron.church/books